This book was edited by Christine Krzystofczyk with assistance from Marcia T. Lucey and Alan J. Hommerding. Design and layout by Christine Enault. Production manager was Deb Johnston. The book was set in Berkeley Oldstyle and Avenir. Printed in Canada.

WLP 017356   ISBN 978-1-58549-576-2

Saved by Beauty

A Spiritual Journey
with Dorothy Day

Michael O'Neill McGrath, OSFS

Foreword by
Robert Ellsberg

Acknowledgments

So many generous people have shared with me their time and their memories of Dorothy Day in the long process of creating this book. I would particularly like to thank the following people. Robert Ellsberg urged me forward from the very first sketches. Patrick and Kathleen Jordan graciously welcomed me into their Staten Island world of place and story. In New York, thanks to Donna Mah and Father Ray Nobiletti, MM, of Transfiguration Church on Mott Street in Chinatown, and the Catholic Workers at St. Joseph House and Maryhouse on the Lower East Side, who let me sketch and drink their coffee. I am grateful to Deborah Kloiber, the archivist of the Ade Bethune collection at St. Catherine's University in St. Paul, Minnesota, and my researchers in all things Salesian, Father Mike Donovan, OSFS, Father Tom Dailey, OSFS, and Sister Mary Grace McCormack, VHM.

I would also like to acknowledge in love and gratitude my Camden family: Susan Cedrone, my landlady, who first brought me to Father Doyle's attention; Joseph Paprzycki, director of the Waterfront South Theater Company, whose reverence for Eugene O'Neill gave me a new perspective on Dorothy's pre-conversion world; and to my beloved fellow Camden confrères, Matt Hillyard, Mike McCue, and Frank Blood, with whom I pray the Office every morning in true Dorothy style. And, saving the best for last, I want to express my loving gratitude to my WLP teammates, the editors and designers who have refined this book into the beautiful gift of praise that it is now: special shout-outs to Christine Krzystofczyk, Marcia Lucey, and Christine Enault.

DEDICATION

For Father Michael Doyle,
pastor of Sacred Heart Church,
who has brought beauty to Camden
brick by brick and heart by heart.

This world in which we live needs beauty in order not to sink into despair. It is beauty, like truth, which brings joy to the [human] heart and is that precious fruit which resists the wear and tear of time, which unites generations and makes them share things in admiration.

—Pope Paul VI

TABLE OF CONTENTS

FOREWORD

Dorothy Day liked to repeat many favorite lines, some from scripture ("What you have done to the least of my brothers and sisters you have done to me"), from the saints ("Where there is no love, put love, and you will draw love out"—St. John of the Cross), or film and literature ("All is grace"—from *The Diary of a Country Priest*). One of her favorite sources was Dostoevsky, especially the words of the holy monk Father Zossima in *The Brothers Karamazov*, who said, "Love in action is a harsh and dreadful thing compared to love in dreams."

Dostoevsky was also the source of one of her favorite lines, one repeated so often that it became almost a personal mantra: "The world will be saved by beauty." Those words resonated with her personally. She herself was saved by beauty.

Readers of her autobiography, *The Long Loneliness*, are familiar with Dorothy's account of the steps leading up to her conversion in 1927. After years of immersion in the struggles for social change and in the tumult of her own personal life, she had experienced much sorrow and confusion: "I had been passing through some years of fret and strife, beauty and ugliness—even some weeks of sadness and despair." But it was not sorrow that turned her heart to God. It was her experience of "natural happiness," living on Staten Island with a man she loved, Forster Batterham, whose intense interest in the natural world lit a spark in her. The simple experience of nature and the goodness of love made her feel she was breathing for the first time: "walking on the beach . . . walking through fields and woods—a new experience for me, which brought me to life, and filled me with joy." Gradually, mysteriously, this experience of natural happiness made

her open to an even greater happiness; her appreciation for the beauty of creation awakened her to the source of beauty. It was at this time that she found herself stopping to pray, and when she discovered that she was pregnant she decided she would have her daughter baptized, a step she would eventually follow, though it meant separating from the adamantly atheist Forster, who would have nothing to do with religion or marriage in any form.

This is part of the story that Mickey McGrath so movingly relates in his loving evocation of Dorothy's life and spirituality. And because he is the first artist to write about her life, it is natural that he picks up on the theme of beauty, which runs like a thread throughout her writings. This theme may surprise those familiar with her life spent among the destitute of New York's slums, or the prophetic witness that brought her to scenes of struggle against violence and injustice, and occasional stints in jail.

Nevertheless, regardless of the circumstances, Dorothy had an eye for beauty: the sight of sunshine on a city tenement, a tree in bloom, a bright poster on an otherwise drab wall, or the picture postcards she liked to collect. (Once, as I was fasting in a jail cell, she sent me one of these cards, an aerial picture of Cape Cod, on which she had written, "I hope this card refreshes you and does not tantalize you.") She revered the work of Catholic Worker artists whose images conveyed what her articles otherwise tried to convey in words: the presence of grace in all things, the belief that the world will be saved by beauty.

The beauty of nature—whether on her retreat on Staten Island or the view of the Hudson River from the Catholic Worker farm—certainly refreshed her soul. But for Dorothy, who always tried to see things in their ultimate perspective, beauty could be found in unexpected places, even in the midst of squalor and disorder. Because of the Incarnation, God had taken on our physical condition. Everything had a sacramental value, if only we had eyes to see. All creation was hallowed. Follow the thread of anything in creation, anything good, any act of generosity or solidarity, and it could lead you to God. Despite all the depredations of industrialism—the noise, the waste, the injustice—she believed that it was necessary to seek out the signs of beauty, the reminders of our Creator, even in the slums. We would be contributing to the misery and desperation of the world "if we failed to rejoice in the sun, the moon, and the stars, in the rivers which surround this island on which we live, in the cool breezes of the bay." And when she searched for beauty, she found it: in "the suffering faces of the poor, in the little trees struggling to survive, in pigeons on the roof across the street, on the rays of sun thru [sic] my windows. By craning my neck I can glimpse the deep blue of sky on sunny days."

It was the counterpart of her effort to put love where there is no love, to see Christ in the "least" of our neighbors, to see the dignity and value in the lives of those who were discarded by society as useless and broken.

Dorothy would have appreciated Mickey's beautiful and sometimes playful images. The early issues of *The Catholic Worker* were largely illustrated by Ade Bethune's depictions of the saints engaged in their everyday work, especially the works of mercy. Mickey's drawings remind us that for all her extraordinary witness, Dorothy Day was a woman of our own world and our own times. Her struggle to follow Christ took place in contexts that remain all too familiar: unemployment and homelessness, war and the struggle for peace, the eternal quest for community and for life in its fullness.

Mickey's celebration of her life is ultimately a challenge to the rest of us—to be braver, more faithful, more loving, to do something to relieve the suffering of those around us. If the world is to be saved, it will be by those who struggle to enlarge the presence of peace and love in the world, to expand the realm of beauty.

—Robert Ellsberg

INTRODUCTORY THOUGHTS

The flowers I present to you are the same; the bouquet I have made of them differs from others because it has been fashioned in a different order and way.

—*Francis de Sales*

We have a "rule of life" that is easy to follow, provided we listen to the wise counsel of such people as St. Teresa [of Ávila] and St. Francis [de Sales]. St. Teresa understood that weariness of the soul. St. Francis tells us to be gentle with ourselves.

—*Dorothy Day*

Visitors to my studio in Camden, New Jersey, are greeted by two painted clay tiles. One depicts Dorothy Day, who holds a steaming cup of coffee as a symbol of hospitality and welcome. The other shows St. Francis de Sales, who sports a beard of flowers instead of the more traditional hair, symbolizing his love of beauty. Hanging on the wall above them is a painting of the Visitation of Mary and Elizabeth, that great Gospel story of two hearts, one older and wiser, the other younger and raring to go, coming together in faith, hope, and love.

One of my favorite aspects of traditional Catholicism is its emphasis on the saints, so I've built an entire ministry around painting them and telling their stories. I've made pilgrimages to saintly shrines and tombs in far-flung places in my restless search for grace and inspiration. But no matter which of God's blessed ones I develop a crush on, such as Dorothy Day, or research for a painting or book, such as Thérèse of Lisieux or Sister Thea Bowman, I always find my way home to St. Francis de Sales, because I haven't yet found anyone else who better understood the twists and tribulations of the human heart, yet remained so joyfully optimistic about it all. How in God's name did he do it, live each present moment of his life with such patience, graciousness, and joie de vivre? And how is it that this giant of the seventeenth-century Church, with all its turbulence and unrest, its Baroque busy-ness and

Reformation zeal, has so much practical down-to-earth wisdom still relevant today? He was all about the little things, the practical steps, the ordinary opportunities we are given to bask in God's presence and maintain inner peace—that's how.

I have become smitten with Dorothy Day because she did the exact same things with her own giant-yet-small life in the twentieth century. I'd always admired and respected her, but my love for her is a very recent development. Until now, I never wanted to grow too close because I was afraid she'd "make me" prove my Christian mettle by moving to the slums with bugs and smelly people drinking lousy coffee. I had been doing exactly what she so famously feared: I had made her a saint so I could easily dismiss her. But as I learned more about her life and read her own writings, I discovered her abiding passion for beauty that made Dorothy more accessible to me as an artist. My primary image of Dorothy Day as a grandmotherly icon of charity ladling out soup and baking bread for poor people was gradually replaced as new images, the ones you see here, came to the foreground. The more I read of her and by her, the more sketches I did—which in turn became a series of painted meditations, which in turn evolved into the book you now hold in your hands.

Meanwhile, in the midst of it all, I moved to Camden, New Jersey. Situated on the Delaware River opposite Philadelphia, Camden is one of the poorest and most dangerous cities in the country. I live there in community with three other Oblates of St. Francis de Sales. I was invited to move my studio there by Father Michael Doyle, renowned pastor of Sacred Heart Church in south Camden. He is called the poet of poverty because he believes, as did Dorothy Day, that beauty heals and transforms the world's sins and pains. Filled with my newfound fervor for all things broken and ugly, how could I not want to work in a parish so centered on beauty as a response to despair?

I truly believe there has been some heavenly conspiracy going on here. Francis de Sales is the patron saint of writers, journalists, and the Catholic press. Dorothy Day was a writer, journalist, and devotee of the saints, including Francis. A few doors down from my studio in Camden are a live theater and a poet's garden, little oases of beauty that not only celebrate the written word, but fly in the face of conventional belief that Camden is beyond repair (more on them later). This trinity of "coincidence" that so presented itself to me couldn't be more obvious: Grace and beauty abound in the most unexpected places, and community and the love of friends help us to discover them. So here we all are on the same pages, conspirators in the Spirit joining hearts and hands to offer the reassuring hope that, in the end, beauty will indeed save the world, just as Dorothy's beloved Dostoevsky once wrote.

The quote from Francis about bouquets is a gentle reminder that in matters of art and spirituality, there really is nothing new under the sun! All artists, all writers, all poets, and all saints merely beg, borrow, and steal from the greats who went before us. Our job, once we find our own voice, is merely to rearrange the flowers they give to us in the way that best suits our own style and temperament. Francis rearranged the flowers from Ávila and Loyola, Thérèse rearranged the flowers from Annecy and Assisi, and Dorothy Day rearranged the flowers from Lisieux. It is my task here to rearrange the flowers that have been presented to me in Camden, New Jersey, from the Bowery in New York. That is exactly the purpose of this book: to reveal generations of faith from the past flowing like a mighty river through the present, leading us together in hope and optimism toward an unknown future.

About Dorothy Day (1897–1980)

Dorothy Day is commonly considered the most influential figure in the American Catholic Church in modern times. She was born in Brooklyn on November 8, 1897, but her family moved to the San Francisco Bay area shortly after when her father, a sports journalist, found work there. The earthquake of 1906 forced the Days to Chicago, where Dorothy lived until she left home for the University of Illinois to study journalism, much to her father's chagrin. Our look at her life in this book begins when she left school in 1916 and moved to New York to work as a reporter.

Dorothy's life journey presents us with one of the great conversion stories of all time. Her embrace of Jesus and his teachings was genuine, profound, and ongoing. Seeing him as the source and epitome of all beauty and truth led her to see him in the poor, the marginalized, and the powerless. The sacraments and traditions of Roman Catholicism, as well as the spiritual truths she found in Russian literature, paved a path of beauty for her along the way. That focus on beauty is the real subject of this book.

As is true with any saint or prophet, Dorothy broke the bounds of religious belief and practice with sheer courage, grace, and creative thinking. She was the major force in leading the American Catholic Church to a deeper understanding of Jesus, the Gospels, and the works of mercy—that these are the things, first and foremost, to which Christians must be obedient. Anything else is secondary.

About St. Francis de Sales (1567–1622)

Since you will be encountering Francis de Sales throughout this book, perhaps meeting him for the very first time, it is only right to tell you a bit about him. He is a gentle giant in Church history. Because his writings and teachings have had such a profound impact on the spiritual life and formation of the Church, he has been named a doctor of the Church. Francis was the bishop of Geneva, the center of Calvinism, at a time when Catholics, dancing, and fun of any kind were outlawed from the city. Since Catholics were not permitted to live there, he operated from his hometown of Annecy, France, a postcard-perfect town in the French Alps just across the border from Switzerland. Together with his best friend and fellow saint, Jane Frances de Chantal, a widowed mother of four, Francis founded the Sisters of the Visitation.

In addition, he was the first true champion of lay spirituality, especially for women, and his writings were directed at that audience. He promoted spiritual direction as a worthwhile practice for everyone, not just religious. He said that no matter who we are or what we do, we can nurture our very own way of devotion to God that springs from the circumstances of our lives. Just as artists have their own unique styles, so do we in our approach to prayer. Francis wrote of these things in his two great works, *The Introduction to the Devout Life* and *Treatise on the Love of God,* which over time became standard required reading in seminaries and religious institutions for centuries.

Though he was born an aristocrat, reared in a castle, and studied law in Paris, Francis de Sales had an abiding love for the poor. He is called the "gentleman saint" because of his impeccable manners and the unfailing respect he showed to all people regardless of their gender, class, or social position. Because of his great humility, he never flaunted his title of bishop or abused his authority. The best way for us to manifest God is through love—the love of self, of spouse, family, friends, community, and even enemies. It is all about love, no more, no less (*nec plus, nec minus*).

Francis' spirituality, called Salesian, is a spirituality of the heart. He had a natural intuition for understanding the intricate workings of the human heart that informed his great devotion to the Sacred Heart of Jesus. His spirituality encourages joyful optimism and inner peace as antidotes to the stresses and anxieties that consume so much of our energy and focus. Three themes that emerge time and again in Salesian spirituality are living life in the present moment; practicing the little virtues, such as humility, patience, and gentleness; and simply being oneself. If you are searching here for the true meaning of life, read no further, because there it is!

The Psalms

This book is arranged in three sections to draw parallels to the psalms, which are prayed throughout the day in the Divine Office, one of the most traditional prayers of the Church. Dorothy prayed the Office every day because of her love for the poetic beauty of the psalms and because she was a Third Order Benedictine. The custom of praying the psalms began in the ancient monasteries and over time became the mandatory daily prayer for all priests. It was uncommon in Dorothy's time for anyone other than priests or religious to pray the Office, but as we will see, doing the uncommon was never a problem for Dorothy.

The first section, which begins with Zechariah's canticle from Morning Prayer, looks at Dorothy's pre-conversion life. Mary's canticle, the Magnificat, is prayed at Evening Prayer and thus sets the tone for the second section, Dorothy's years at the Catholic Worker. The third section starts off with Simeon's canticle from Night Prayer and leads us into Dorothy's twilight years.

May these images and stories of St. Francis de Sales, Dorothy Day, and Camden, New Jersey, touch the lonely places in your heart. May the light-hearted paintings ease your burdens with the healing grace of joy. May the psalms that are featured at the close of each segment connect your heart to the hearts of other seekers of God across time and space.

Prologue:
On Pilgrimage

Staten Island and the Lower East Side of Manhattan are the destination spots for Dorothy Day devotees and pilgrims. While I've been to New York City countless times in my life, I'd never gone with the intention of seeing New York through Dorothy's eyes. I know it would have been much easier to do photo research on the Internet, but the easy way out would never do for a true pilgrim. I wouldn't walk the same cracked pavements or sandy beaches on which Dorothy stepped with journalistic attentiveness or prayerful devotion. I'd never soak up the very same golden sunlight sliding down the soaring skyscrapers of lower Manhattan or rocking gently on the silvery surface of Raritan Bay, which Dorothy faced while typing at her desk. I wouldn't feel the frenetic energy of the streets or see the stressed beauty etched on the faces of rushing passersby. A true pilgrim, like any artist or journalist, leaves no stone unturned in the search for God.

My idea of pilgrimage is grabbing a sketchbook and a healthy supply of pens and heading out to wherever the Spirit calls. For me, sketching is praying. It is a direct connection to the place or saint I am visiting because I have no better way of truly entering the present moment. While I draw, nothing else is more important than what is before my eyes—whether I am contemplating a vast open landscape or the tiny details of stained glass over a cathedral side altar, the crowds in a busy airport, or the coffee cup (or beer glass) on the table before me. No matter what is going on around me, my roaming pilgrim eyes discover God in the details, and sometimes the devil too, and when God happens, ordinary little things take on the most extraordinary significance.

I was blessed with two special pilgrim guides on my first Staten Island pilgrimage, Patrick and Kathleen Jordan. They met and fell in love with each other at the Catholic Worker in New York, where they also formed a lifelong friendship with Dorothy. They raised their kids at Spanish Camp on the beach of Raritan Bay, living in the cottage across the narrow lane from Dorothy's. And in addition to becoming instant friends, they also proved to be the most generous and thoughtful pilgrim guides a roving artist could want when they gave me a full Staten Island tour of all sites related to Dorothy and shared their memories of her.

As we walked the very beach where Dorothy loved to sit and be her contemplative self in her last years, when her life had at long last slowed down, Patrick recalled that as a native Californian who grew up near the gorgeous beaches of the Pacific Ocean, he initially had great difficulty seeing the beauty of this somewhat unmemorable, debris-strewn beach that Dorothy so loved. It took him a long time to let go of his own expectations and see it through her eyes, he told me as we stepped over the occasional soda can or potato chip bag amid the driftwood and shells.

I was sketching as he relayed this story when out of the blue—and on cue—a snow-white swan appeared from behind the tall grasses of the marsh alongside the beach, gliding silently in circles across the surface of the water. It was for each of us, stunned as we were into momentary silence, a fleeting glimpse of the sacred. (Pilgrims, you see, don't believe in mere coincidence.) We watched without speaking as this most graceful of all creatures floated into and then out of view, disappearing into the meandering course of the slow tide.

"Patrick," I asked when the moment had passed and it seemed okay to speak, "do you think we just had a visitation from Dorothy?" His affirmative reply was all the reassurance I needed to trust my instincts—that not only had we just entered one of the thin places where the sacred meets the ordinary, but that this project, with all its paintings and research and as yet unwritten text, was indeed meant to be. Who am I to doubt God, the source of all beauty, or to deny the Holy Spirit? Why would I want to run from grace or block the blessings that constantly tumble my way, usually unbidden, often unnoticed? Every moment of our lives is brimful of grace, and as Dorothy Day and her fellow saintly pilgrims remind us, we shouldn't want to miss a single one. We should, as Thomas Merton used to say, keep our eyes clean.

PART I
ZECHARIAH'S CANTICLE

And you, child, will be called prophet of the Most High
   for you will go before the Lord to prepare God's ways,
to give God's people knowledge of salvation.

(Luke 1:76–77a)

TENEMENTS

Serve God where you are and do what you are doing.
—*Francis de Sales*

Because God has given me writing to do as a vocation, I write.
—*Dorothy Day*

In 1916, after dropping out of college in Illinois, Dorothy started her career as a journalist working for a socialist paper in New York. What the writer Dorothy so trenchantly described in her autobiography as life on the Lower East Side was a horror show: dark and evil-smelling hallways, tile floors usually slimy with filth, the foul odor of decaying garbage, the fetid odor from the dark hallways, bedbugs. She wrote about starvation, disease, and bread riots in the streets of New York. She got caught up in all the various social causes, covering strikes and picket lines, demonstrations and protests, feeling an affinity for socialism, union rights, and anarchism. She was sympathetic to Communism, but never joined the party. Because of it all, she would choose slum living for the rest of her life. "If one must dwell in cities," she wrote, "I prefer the slums of the poor to the slums of the rich."

At the time she covered the Lower East Side, the largest immigrant groups were Jews from Eastern Europe who lived and worked in squalor. Workshops in this, the world's largest garment industry, were often set up in the tiny living rooms of overcrowded and filthy tenement apartments. Several years after the infamous Triangle Shirtwaist Factory fire, the nation was looking more seriously at workers' rights, labor laws, and women's suffrage—all issues for which Dorothy had great passion. She was a young woman in what was very much a man's world, discovering her vocation as a writer and activist.

If you look closely at the details of the painting on the next page that came out of my own visit to the Lower East Side, you can see Dorothy doing her journalist thing, her typewriter perched on a trash can, observing the details of this multi-cultured world that inflamed a passion in her for the poor working classes, that filled her with devotion for the neglected masses who struggled on the margins of society. She was finding her voice among those who were literally shouting for their lives at raucous political rallies or on crowded streets. While it was a painfully lonely time in her life, a time of hard work with little rest or financial benefit, it was also thrilling and transformative because she was discovering her life's passion.

I walked the streets in solitude and my heart wept within me for the ugliness I saw. . . .

When I was in the subway, I felt closed in, trapped. When I walked the narrow streets of lower New York through the tenement districts I felt that I was caught, that never again would I be happy or free.

But Dorothy wrote of hidden beauty as well: of the beauty of unbreakable family ties and children of different nationalities playing together in the streets, of classical music on her Victrola, of the smell of fresh bread from bakery shops, of people generously sharing with each other what little they had. Look more closely at the painting and you will see Jesus standing on the fire escape far above her head, watching over all she surveys. She wasn't ready to see him at this point in time or hear his voice in the noisy clatter, but he was there nonetheless, keeping a watchful eye and paving the way to her future. God's grace was already at work in her; she just didn't know it yet.

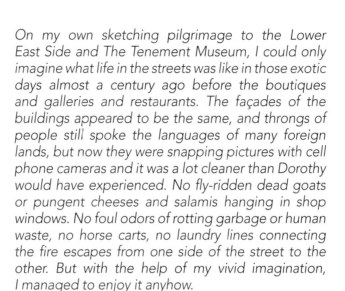

On my own sketching pilgrimage to the Lower East Side and The Tenement Museum, I could only imagine what life in the streets was like in those exotic days almost a century ago before the boutiques and galleries and restaurants. The façades of the buildings appeared to be the same, and throngs of people still spoke the languages of many foreign lands, but now they were snapping pictures with cell phone cameras and it was a lot cleaner than Dorothy would have experienced. No fly-ridden dead goats or pungent cheeses and salamis hanging in shop windows. No foul odors of rotting garbage or human waste, no horse carts, no laundry lines connecting the fire escapes from one side of the street to the other. But with the help of my vivid imagination, I managed to enjoy it anyhow.

At Sacred Heart Church, as in many parishes around the country, it is the custom on Good Friday to pray the Stations of the Cross while processing through the streets of the neighborhood. Pairs of people take turns carrying the cross from one station to the next. Each stop on this Way of the Cross directs our prayerful attention to some significant social or political reality. Some sites are holy ground where murders have occurred or bodies have been found.

LORD, you have probed me, you know me;
You know when I sit and stand;
You understand my thoughts from afar.
(Psalm 139:1–2)

2   Jail and the Rivers of Babylon

To change the world we must change ourselves.

—Francis de Sales

You cannot pace the floor of a barred cell, or lie on your back on a hard cot watching a gleam of sunlight travel slowly, oh, so slowly, across the room, without coming to the realization that until the heart and soul of a man is changed, there is no hope of happiness for him.

—Dorothy Day

Dorothy was jailed and brutalized in Washington while demonstrating in front of the White House for women's right to vote; had two ribs cracked at a peace rally in Baltimore opposing World War I; and did a second stint in jail in Chicago, arrested on trumped-up charges of living in a brothel that was in actuality a boarding house for political activists. Later in life, she went to jail for ignoring civil defense drills in the fifties, and for demonstrating against the Vietnam War in the sixties and for farm workers' rights in the seventies. In every instance, she was more appalled by the cruel behavior of the guards and matrons than by the prostitutes and drug addicts with whom she was incarcerated and whom she found to be generally kind and non-judgmental. One time a madam, assuming that Dorothy was in jail for the same reason as she, sought to reassure her by pointing out that there always had to be a first time.

Perhaps you've heard Irish charm described as the ability to tell someone to go to hell in such a way that they look forward to the trip. I've always believed that's a good definition of art. The creative acts of writing, composing, or painting are the best means we humans have of looking pain and suffering right in the eye and declaring ourselves free of their power over us. I am reminded of that in *The Long Loneliness*, in which Dorothy wrote about her first experience of being arrested and jailed while demonstrating for women's rights in front of the White House. She describes being transported by train from a prison to a workhouse in Occoquan, Virginia:

> We were ushered by a number of police-women into a waiting train which rolled out of the station immediately, the lamps along the road had not yet been lit. It was the beginning of November, and I sat with

my face pressed against the glass watching the blue twilight, pierced with the black shapes of many scrawny trees. Here and there lamps glowed in farmhouse windows. In the west the sky still held the radiance of the sun which faded gradually and left one with a terrible sense of desolation and loneliness. It was sadly beautiful at that time of night.

You can almost hear the haunting whistle of the train slowly clickety-clacking its way through the moonlit fields of northern Virginia. As the quip about blarney suggests, it is what great writers and poets do: they make beautifully worded sense of life's chaos and trauma. She

held on to that present-moment experience of heightened awareness and vividly depicted it many years later. By then, the memory had been healed and had lost its power to keep her stuck in the past. Writing about it enabled her to see it from a different perspective and helped her to keep going, just as it had done thousands of years before for the composers of the psalms.

Because the Bible was the only reading material allowed in detention, Dorothy read the psalms over and over—a practice she would continue every day for the rest of her life once she discovered the Liturgy of the Hours following her conversion. The psalms can touch our hearts as no other prayer can when we face tragic events or troublesome circumstances. They reached Dorothy across time and place, touching mysterious chords of hope within her and a vivid sense of longing for the sacred. The rivers of Babylon and the railroad tracks of Virginia became one.

The psalms speak in a timeless way to the human heart because they are about the human heart in all its broken glory. Whether writing about the Babylonian captivity, enslavement in Egypt, or the sheer delight of God's love, the composers of the psalms did what writers, poets, and mystics have always done across time and culture. They embrace the mystery of life and reveal the hidden beauty of the human spirit. They encourage us to hang in there, advise us not to be afraid, remind us we are never alone, and teach us that all will be well. No matter the prisons in which we find ourselves, especially the ones of our own making, the psalms can set our hearts free.

Because she knew firsthand what it was like to be incarcerated, Dorothy loved to gather a group of Christmas carolers to sing outside the women's jail in New York City.

By the rivers of Babylon
*   we sat mourning and weeping*
*   when we remembered Zion.*
On the poplars of that land
*   we hung up our harps.*
There our captors asked us
*   for the words of a song;*
Our tormentors, for a joyful song:
*   "Sing for us a song of Zion!"*
But how could we sing a song of the Lord
*   in a foreign land?*

(Psalm 137:1–4)

In the Hell Hole with the Hound of Heaven

During the night we must pray for the light.

—*Francis de Sales*

Where sin abounds, grace abounds doubly.

—*Dorothy Day*

Artists, writers, and bohemian types of all stripes throughout history have gravitated toward favorite "watering holes" where they could discuss their work, exchange ideas, and drink way too much for their own good. Our twenty-year-old struggling journalist and writer was no exception when she discovered The Golden Swan, aka the Hell Hole, a real old-fashioned dive—replete with gangsters, hookers, Communists, and cheap gin—on the corner of Fourth Street and Sixth Avenue in Greenwich Village. It was one of her favorite places to unwind as she set out to write the great American novel.

The years leading up to the Jazz Age of the Roaring Twenties were an exciting and tumultuous time in American art and literature, a creative period of breaking the rules and finding new ways to express the spiritual angst and rootlessness of the modern world. The Hell Hole was one of the important incubators in American culture where these new ideas were nurtured.

The bar owner was a retired Irish boxer named Tom Wallace and the bartender rejoiced in the intriguing nickname of "Lefty Louie." John Sloan, one of the renowned painters of the Ashcan School of art, had a studio on the block. Two other great modern artists, Charles Demuth and Marsden Hartley, both members of Alfred Stieglitz's gallery (he the father of modern photography and husband of Georgia O'Keeffe),

their shared concern for the plight of the poor and working classes. Dorothy later wrote that, in the throes of his drunken misery, Gene, who had abandoned the practice of Catholicism at fifteen, could recite from memory *The Hound of Heaven*, a classic poem of one hundred eighty-one lines by Francis Thompson about the human heart's attempts to run and hide from God, symbolized by a hound on the hunt for a human soul. The poem spoke to her deeply held sense of being "haunted by God" in ways she couldn't name.

At the same time, Dorothy was growing increasingly aware of feeling some vague spiritual stirrings. Often, as she stumbled home from the Hell Hole at dawn, she would stop in St. Joseph's Church on Sixth Avenue (now called the Avenue of the Americas), where she would sneak into the back pew and simply observe the crowd at the 5:30 morning Mass. Ignorant of what was really going on up front, she was always moved by the devotion of the worshipers, who were mostly women on their way to work. This mysterious sense of holiness and beauty found its way into the darker recesses of her heart.

The sordid side of the Hell Hole took its toll on Dorothy, however, when a tragic event set her on a new course. One night, a young man named Louis Holladay, who had just been jilted by his fiancée, committed suicide by overdosing

shared a shanty apartment across the street with Communist activist John Reed, his wife, Louise Bryant, and an up-and-coming playwright named Eugene O'Neill.

Dorothy chain-smoked cigarettes she rolled herself (a habit she gave up in the thirties) and bought rounds of cheap whiskey for her friends while going from table to table singing "Frankie and Johnnie Were Lovers," much to the delight of Gene, who was taken with how lovely she looked in candlelight. She was intelligent, pretty, vivacious, and loved being one of the guys—especially since those guys were either literary types and political activists like herself, or actors from Gene's theater troupe, the Provincetown Players, who would crowd into the bar following their rehearsals and performances. In her later autobiographies, she wrote that "no one ever wanted to go to bed, no one ever wanted to be alone." The Hell Hole filled Dorothy's need for community.

At the time he and Dorothy met in 1917, Gene was on his way to becoming a brilliant writer, tortured by his tragic past and drowning his sorrows night after night over ill-fated romance and memories he could neither heal nor banish. Dorothy and Gene would go for midnight walks through the streets of New York and discuss life, love, the existence of God, and

on heroin in full view of those present. While everyone else ran from the bar in fear, Dorothy and Charles Demuth stayed with him until the police arrived. Dorothy cradled the man's dead body in her arms and hid the empty vial in her pocket so his death would appear a heart attack to the police. The horror of this event forced Dorothy to take a good penetrating look at her life and the direction it was headed.

Who in the world could have imagined in those dark glory days and smoky nights that the hard-drinking, chain-smoking reporter with anarchist tendencies and the struggling playwright who sat next to her, the two crying in their cups and offering toasts to misery, were destined for monumental greatness? Not even they could have. Life in the Hell Hole, short-lived as it was, introduced Dorothy to her own inner shadows, which not only fed her writing skills but led her bit by slow bit, step by small step, to the lifelong process of conversion, with the ever loyal Hound of Heaven leading the way.

Sadly, Eugene O'Neill never found inner peace or freedom from alcoholism and his bitter past, but he did beat the swords of his torment into ploughshares of beauty and truth. He became America's greatest playwright and changed the course of the American theater. He won four Pulitzer Prizes and was the first American to win the Nobel Prize for writing. The Hell Hole inspired the bar setting he would later create for *The Iceman Cometh*. A character named Charles Marsden in *A Strange Interlude* was inspired by his old roommates, the artists Charles Demuth and Marsden Hartley.

One of the many themes running through O'Neill's masterpiece, *Long Day's Journey into Night*, is about time, about how our present is tied to our past and future. The bleakness of his own childhood in a troubled and tragic family tortured him all his days, but he turned that angst into works of epic beauty. Just read these magnificent words from a soliloquy near the end of the play. Through the character of Edmund Tyrone, O'Neill recalls a heightened awareness of

God that he once experienced on a ship when he was a restless young man roaming the world in search of peace:

> I became drunk with the beauty and singing rhythm of it, and for a moment I lost myself—actually lost my life. I was set free! . . . I dissolved in the sea, became white sails and flying spray, became beauty and rhythm, became moonlight and the ship and the high dim-starred sky! I belonged, without past or future, within peace and unity and a wild joy, within something greater than my own life, or the life of Man, to life itself! To God, if you want to put it that way.

While he no longer practiced his faith, Gene, like Dorothy, was searching for God. The incarnational theology of Catholicism with all the beauty of its words and images helped him to find creative redemption in the midst of tragedy and addiction. It is at the heart of Jesus' teachings: "No one has greater love than this, to lay down one's life for one's friends" (John 15:13). Eugene O'Neill did exactly that when he ventured into the lonely tenements of his soul and through beautiful words and tragic stories empowered others to do the same. He made great works of art from his pain, and in doing so, became a wounded healer. God's grace is ever at work, even in the tortured soul and drunken ramblings of a doubter.

All which I took from thee I did but take,
    Not for thy harms,
But just that thou might'st seek it in My arms.
      —*The Hound of Heaven*

For the rest of her life, Dorothy remembered Gene in her prayers with "love and pain." She prayed for him at Mass in 1956 in his "black despair and tragic death," and she prayed the Office of the Dead for him and his son Shane, who committed suicide in 1977, the second of his sons to do so.

The End of the Hell Hole

Realizing that her life needed to take a less self-destructive path, Dorothy re-invented herself, and for a year became a nurse at a county hospital in Brooklyn to help with the severe nursing shortage created by World War I and the great flu epidemic of 1918. She loved serving the poor and felt that nursing was the noblest profession a woman could find. She also fell in love with an orderly named Lionel Moise, by whom she became pregnant. He didn't want the baby, and overwhelmed by fear of losing him, she had an abortion. Later in life, Dorothy would say it was the most regrettable thing she ever did, but she didn't wallow in guilt and misery about it. The abortion and the experience of clinging to a man who was no good for her (he left her) were tough life lessons that taught her about forgiveness of self and compassion for others. She learned there is nothing so dark and hateful in our lives that God can't penetrate with the light of tender mercy. Dorothy always held a special place in her heart for women struggling with unplanned pregnancies and reached out to them with compassion.

Over the next couple of years, Dorothy was briefly married to a man with whom she toured London, Paris, and the Isle of Capri; returned to Chicago, where she worked at a series of jobs including clerk at Montgomery Ward, artist's model, and journalist, plus did a second stint in jail; and then moved to New Orleans, where, working as a "girl reporter," she made frequent visits to the cathedral and prayed with a rosary given to her by a Jewish Communist friend. Finally, she returned to New York and bought a cottage on Staten Island, where the Hound of Heaven patiently awaited her arrival.

As the deer longs for streams of water,
so my soul longs for you, O God.
(Psalm 42:2)

Down the corner from my studio resides the South Camden Theater Company. Started in the basement of Sacred Heart Church, it is now housed in what was once a thriving corner bar called Walt's Café. Walt's grandson, Joe Paprzycki, a playwright and the theater's director, joined forces with Father Michael Doyle to create this vibrant space for live theater, the first of its kind in the country. It is one of the chief reasons I moved to Camden, to be part of this community reclaiming the city through beauty and culture.

This painting of Dorothy and Eugene at the Hell Hole was blessed by Bishop Joseph Gallante during a most special evening of prayer and drama, then installed in the lobby, its permanent home.

STATEN ISLAND: IN LOVE WITH LIFE

The truest happiness to be found in this life is when we are satisfied with what is sufficient.

—Francis de Sales

All my life I have been haunted by God.

*—Dorothy Day
quoting Dostoevsky*

As I begin to write this section, I am staying at a generous friend's condo on the bay side of Stone Harbor, a New Jersey ocean resort. Just across the way from my balcony are row upon row of boats shrink-wrapped for the winter in white plastic blankets and stacked like firewood. The March air feels bitter cold, the water looks icy frigid, but the sun shines brightly and the seagulls go sailing by. I am listening to a playlist of opera arias I created just for this occasion, and waiting for water to boil for tea. I have just come in from a walk on the very windswept beach where I was too cold to bend over and pick up the shells that caught my eye (or, alternatively, I'm just lazy). "There will always be more where they came from," I decided as I walked briskly over the sand dunes to head home. It is Ash Wednesday, by the way, and all this cold beauty, this feast for the senses that surrounds me, takes my mind off fasting and puts my heart there instead.

With money she made from a novel called *The Eleventh Virgin*, Dorothy bought a cottage on the beach of Staten Island and began what she considered one of the happiest times of her life. Instead of political rallies and protests, she was now writing more about "seagulls . . . diving with a splash into the shallow gray water for a fish" and "mussels garlanded in seaweed." She loved walking the beach and conversing with her neighbors, the fishermen and beachcombers who lived in shacks nearby. She set up her writing desk by the window so she could look out at the water and be inspired by the steady rhythm of the waves. She was finding her voice as a writer and feeling the urge to pray, discovering inner peace in the process. Most of all, she was learning the difference between seeking pleasure and finding true happiness.

The simple life introduced Dorothy to her contemplative side. In the country, away from the commotion of city life and the distraction of friends or political rallies, she was not only seeing herself more clearly, she was learning to love who she saw. She found herself serenely drawn to nature, resting in the stillness of salt air breezes and clouds rolling over Raritan Bay. She neither dwelled on her past nor fretted about the future. She fully entered the present moment of her simple life on Staten Island and met her true self for the first time. In an article she wrote in 1931 for *Commonweal* magazine entitled "Now We Are Home Again," Dorothy beautifully describes her sense of coming home after being away for several years:

> Just beyond my little lawn and the wild cherry and apple trees, the ground dips sharply to the sands which are as yellow and as warm as ever. The bay is a calm gray blue, and the little waves chuckle along the beach. . . . I am very glad to be home again, to be cultivating my own bit of soil, to be living in my own house and to feel for the time at least, that I am never going to leave it again. There is beauty here too, a lovely, gentle beauty of cultivated gardens, and woodlands, and shore.

As any creative spirit can tell you, there is a big difference between loneliness and being alone. I have come to know that I am more likely to feel lonely when I am with a crowd of strangers than when I am by myself. That's because being alone and quiet allows me to concentrate on listening in a creative way to the still, small voice within. Being still in nature is an added bonus. I paint and write and think better when I am alone and calm. In fact, I crave it because when I am engaged in doing what I love to do more than anything else, I am aware of God's presence in a way I can't be with the distraction of people and preoccupations.

It seems counter-intuitive, but the best time to go on retreat is when you are up to your eyeballs in deadlines or obligations coming at you from every side (especially if you can't imagine life without your cell phone!). I have made and/or directed many retreats over the years in a variety of settings and venues—deserts, woods, mountains, and seashores. What I have come to learn is this: where you go to get away is not as important as that you go. Treat yourself to a time of listening to the still, small voice of God within you. If you can't do a whole week or even a weekend, go for just half a day. Alone. Without a laptop, cell phone, or credit card. Just sit back and wait for wonder to appear. And when it does, just keep it to yourself—don't text someone to tell them about it!

One thing I ask of the LORD;
  this I seek:
To dwell in the LORD'*s house*
  all the days of my life,
To gaze on the LORD'*s beauty,*
  to visit [God's] temple.

(Psalm 27:4)

I drew this scene of the Philadelphia skyline from the front seat of my car on a cold winter day. A small fishing pier named for Father Michael Doyle offers one of the best views of the city on the other side of the Delaware River. After I sketched it, I spent the rest of that winter afternoon painting it in my studio—a mini-retreat for sure.

Forster Batterham: Dorothy's Song of Songs

Our faith should be naked and simple.

—*Francis de Sales*

The very love of Nature and study of her secrets which is bringing me to faith, separates him from religion.

—*Dorothy Day*

In the midst of her idyllic life on Staten Island, Dorothy fell deeply in love with Forster Batterham, an atheist anarchist who had an abundance of scientific curiosity and a deep distrust of any and all such institutions as church or marriage. He didn't work much, preferring a life devoted to fishing and charting the stars and watching birds, all of which he eagerly shared with Dorothy, who was totally enchanted by the newness of it all—and him. They entered into a common-law marriage, and for a while life was good.

> If breath is life, then I was beginning to be full of it because of him. I was filling my lungs with it, walking on the beach, resting on the pier beside him while he fished, rowing with him in the calm bay, walking through fields and woods—a new experience entirely for me, one which brought me to life, and filled me with joy.

Ironically, it was this love of creation that Forster nurtured in her that led her to God, the source of all that beauty. She frequently found herself praying spontaneously because she was so happy with life for the first time, but couldn't talk with him about it because of his antagonistic attitude toward religious faith. The age-old battle between science and religion intruded in their relationship as Dorothy's urges to pray grew deeper and more frequent. She sometimes directed her prayers toward a statue of Mary she had been given as a housewarming gift from an artist friend. She prayed the rosary, even not knowing the "proper" way to do it, because it gave her inner peace.

Dorothy was experiencing equally strong tugs of physical and spiritual longing, the same tension at the heart of the Song of Songs, one of the greatest mystical poems of all time. Found in the Hebrew Testament of the Bible, it is a beautiful dialogue between God and humanity symbolized by the passionate, erotic relationship of two lovers. It is a feast for artists, with its images of a man and woman chasing each other naked through a garden, leaping like gazelles, and an equally bountiful feast for Christian mystics such as St. Bernard of Clairvaux and St. Francis de Sales, who were drawn to its expression of God's passionate love for us.

In the Catholic Salesian tradition, the Song of Songs is seen as a metaphor for the marriage of Christ and the Church. In very poetic ways, it teaches us that all human hearts are touched by desire to know and love God, and that we are most aware of that divine or sacred love through our human relationships. If we truly believe we are made in the image and likeness of God, then we must believe that we are spiritual as well as physical beings. Sex is seen as a spiritual act, a sign of mutual trust and respect. Intuitively, Dorothy was beginning to grasp this, while Forster never could, nor would he.

He stayed out late on the pier fishing, and came in smelling of seaweed and salt air; getting into bed, cold with the chill November air, he held me close to him in

On my bed at night I sought him
   whom my heart loves—
    I sought him but did not find him.
I will rise then and go about the city;
   in the streets and crossings I will seek
Him whom my heart loves.
   When I found him whom my heart loves
I took hold of him and would not let him go.
        (Song of Songs 3:1–2, 4bc)

silence. I loved him in every way, as a wife, as a mother, even. I loved him for all he knew and pitied him for all he didn't know. I loved him for the odds and ends I had to fish out of his sweater pockets and for the sand and shells he brought in with his fishing. I loved his lean cold body as he got into bed smelling of the sea, and I loved his integrity and stubborn pride . . . It was killing me to think of leaving him.

It took several more years of arguing and splitting up and desperate attempts to keep things together before Dorothy could accept the heartbreaking reality that their relationship had no chance of survival because her heart belonged to another. It would indeed be in the streets and crossings of the city that Dorothy would soon take hold of her One True Love and never let go. She was transformed by the suffering of her broken heart and in the process found broader, deeper, purer love that lasted her entire lifetime.

If Dorothy hadn't discovered within herself the courage and resolve to leave Forster, as unbearably heartbreaking as it was, and accept that he wasn't the true source of her fulfillment and self-esteem, as she so passionately wished him to be, she would never have become the true "Dorothy Day" she was meant to be for the world. It is interesting to ponder the person she may have become had she stayed with him. It is interesting for us to ponder who we would be today if we hadn't made the tough choices that we knew deep down were better than the easy ones—when we let common sense prevail over our emotions.

My tears have become my food day and night,
and they ask daily, "Where is your God?"

(Psalm 42:4)

6 MOTHERHOOD AND CONVERSION

Just as an expectant mother prepares cradle, linen and swaddling clothes . . . so also our Lord's bounty is heavy and fruitful with you.

—Francis de Sales

A conversion is a lonely experience. We do not know what is going on in the depths of the heart and soul of another. We scarcely know ourselves.

—Dorothy Day

Except for St. Paul, who while traveling down the road and minding his own business was blinded by a bolt of lightning and heard the booming voice of God telling him he'd better straighten the hell out, I've always been skeptical about the born-again notion of instant conversion. My experience tells me that true conversion, to be deep and authentic, takes a lifetime—that it's a journey of ongoing, unfolding discovery and that we are pilgrims on that journey. And as every cliché-dropping pilgrim since *The Canterbury Tales* can tell you, life is all about the journey, not the destination. Becoming a mother set Dorothy on an entirely new pilgrim path. She said it brought her not only unsurpassable joy, but also the need to worship and adore God.

Tamar Teresa was born on March 3, 1927. Determined that her child not live the restless and orderless life she herself had been living, Dorothy had her baby baptized in the Catholic Church after consulting a Sister of Charity who lived nearby.

Sister Aloysia was the catechist who taught Dorothy the basics of the Catholic religion, visiting her in her cottage three days a week. She gave her pious books on the saints, drilled her on the catechism questions she assigned for homework, and even managed some criticism of her housekeeping skills. But Dorothy's real lessons in the faith came from the love and suffering of life, and that mysterious Hound of Heaven who had haunted her since she was a girl.

Forster was not pleased and life with him grew increasingly torturous until he finally left her for good.

When Dorothy was baptized in 1927 and made her first confession and Communion right after, it was not a particularly joyful occasion. She didn't regret it, but she was still full of inner conflict and such nagging questions as, "What in God's name am I doing?" It was neither the official beginning of her faith journey, negating everything in her life prior to that moment, nor

scandalous behavior of some Church leaders and members. But one thing she would never lose was her radical spirit.

God, who has all the time in the world, is always waiting for us as we stumble our way through life. Dorothy Day's life and writings point us to this ever patient, ever loving God who dwells within. All of her life, she had felt haunted by God, vaguely aware of a divine and mysterious presence. Like most of us, it took Dorothy a long, long time to accept and embrace fully the love of God that is freely given and abundant, that doesn't judge or discriminate, that places on us no expectations save gratitude. It is a lifelong process, this willingness to be carried along. It is the pilgrim's journey. It is why for decades Dorothy Day chose "On Pilgrimage" as the name of her column in *The Catholic Worker* newspaper.

Conversion is a gradual accumulation of momentary flashes of enlightenment, "Aha!" moments of self-discovery, sometimes joyful, sometimes unsettling. It is in our struggles with these that our hearts of stone are turned to hearts of flesh. Dorothy changed from thinking she couldn't live without Forster to realizing she couldn't live with him once she opened her heart to all the other, better options that were laid out before her—especially her new baby girl and the Church they had both just entered.

was it an ending, as if some final goal had at long last been achieved. It was the centerpiece of her long conversion pilgrimage. Dorothy initially embraced the Church because it revealed Christ to her through the beauty of the saints and sacraments. In the process she lost the man she loved and the support of all her radical friends, none of whom could see past the sometimes

Rather, I have stilled my soul,
hushed it like a weaned child.
Like a weaned child on its mother's lap,
so is my soul within me.

(Psalm 131:2)

7 Hooray for Hollywood

Change of place helps to ease the pains of grief or love.
—*Francis de Sales*

We do not pick the particular kind of suffering we want to bear.
—*Dorothy Day*

Have you ever, in your wildest dreams, considered Dorothy Day and Hollywood in the same breath? It takes quite a leap of the imagination, doesn't it? But the fact remains: Dorothy Day headed for Hollywood in September of 1929, the dawn of its "Golden Age," with her baby and a few months' contract for work with Pathé Studios in her arms. She herself didn't make much of it in her later autobiography, but this tiny, meaningless, insignificant, hardly-worth-mentioning blip on the radar of her life was the seedling that grew into this book.

From the moment I first read of it, before I learned the whole story behind it, my overactive imagination churned out cartoons by the dozens as I pondered the "patron saint" of peace and justice, the very icon of the works of mercy, bumping into platinum-haired starlets on Rodeo Drive or touring the studio back lots with dancing chorus girls, gun-slinging cowboys, and tough-talking gangsters. I probably spent more days curled up on the couch watching Turner Classic Movies (for research, but fun) than she did in her entire time in California. Alas, almost all of the work I labored over with such blood, sweat, and tears has ended up on the

cutting room floor—where, I grudgingly admit, it belongs. That's show biz for you.

Here's what really happened. One day, while she was doing the dishes and probably crying over Forster, she received a phone call from a Hollywood studio, offering her a contract to do some writing for them because she was going to be the next Dostoevsky. It was the perfect storm of opportunities. Not only was she being recognized as a promising writer, it also meant steady work for her, an unemployed single mother. And best of all, it was as far away from Forster as she could get in the continental United States. So she and

Tamar hopped a train for California, the land of golden opportunity, in search of a new dream to replace the Forster one that obviously hadn't panned out.

Dorothy hated every blessed minute of it. Not, as you may be tempted to think, because it was a Sodom and Gomorrah teeming with sin and vice—like the Hell Hole, only sunnier; not because it was a materialistic wasteland of designer gowns and luxury cars; not because it was a spiritually bankrupt business that treated people like property. It was because she was bored to tears! The studio simply didn't come through with the work promised to her and the other writers they'd hired. She sat in her office all day reading lousy scripts and developing her own ideas for stories while staring at the

swimming pool and geraniums outside her office window. She was also desperately lonely and still consumed by forlorn hopes of hanging on to Forster, as her letters to him indicate.

In those letters, she described Hollywood as deplorable, ugly, barren, and suburban. Even the beach was unspeakably dreary. She was blue as indigo, she wrote, and felt nothing but loneliness. (She did observe, on a positive note, that the movie studios were magnificent.) She also said that since she could never marry anyone else, his pigheadedness was condemning her to a life of celibacy. Even her newfound religious faith was not yet a great source of comfort. She "practiced" it and prayed often, but it hadn't yet touched her depths.

Hollywood was the spiritual desert place where, like the Samaritan woman at the well, Dorothy came face to face with a lifetime of her restless searchings: going to college at a time when most women didn't; dropping out of said college; investigative reporting in the slums of New York punctuated by a few stints in jail; carousing at the Hell Hole; an abortion and unfulfilling affairs; a rebound marriage to a man she never talked about again; shattered dreams of a career as a novelist; a common-law marriage to a man who couldn't begin to understand or accept her; baptism into

YOU MY CHILD SHALL BE CALLED THE PROPHET OF THE MOST HIGH, FOR YOU WILL GIVE PEOPLE KNOWLEDGE OF SALVATION BY THE FORGIVENESS OF THEIR SINS.

a faith she didn't quite yet comprehend and that alienated her friends; and unwed motherhood. Other than that, she had it all together.

Disillusioned with Hollywood's false allures, Dorothy left town when her contract was up. Still not ready to face the temptations of Forster back home in New York, she made her way with Tamar to Mexico to see if Our Lady of Guadalupe had any suggestions for a new sense of purpose and meaning in her life. While there, she wrote some articles for the Catholic journal *Commonweal*, beginning a professional relationship that would last until the end of her life. By the time she returned home to

New York, she was a very different person, free of Forster and ready to fill the void with something new.

We all need a desert place to call our own, a place far from home, or at least as far as we can manage, where alone and undistracted we can see our life and all its craziness for what it is: a grace-filled journey from struggle to abundance. Hollywood and Mexico were the deserts where Dorothy was brought to the depths of her misery, where she discovered hints of a well within leaping up with joy, where she began the upward climb to a redemption whose time had come.

Where can I hide from your spirit?
    From your presence, where can I flee?
If I ascend to the heavens, you are there.
If I fly with the wings of dawn
    and alight beyond the sea,
Even there your hand will guide me,
    your right hand hold me fast.

                    (Psalm 139:7–8a, 9–10)

PETER MAURIN

Let us be who we are and be it well.

—Francis de Sales

I was a journalist, I loved to write, but I was far better at making criticism of the social order than making any constructive ideas in relation to it. Peter had a program . . . he opened our minds to great horizons, he gave us a vision.

—Dorothy Day

The Buddhists have a saying: "When the student is ready, the teacher appears." That is literally what happened to Dorothy one day when a total stranger named Peter Maurin knocked on her door. She had just returned from Washington, D.C., where she had gone to cover a hunger march for *Commonweal*. While there she stopped at the National Shrine on the feast of the Immaculate Conception and prayed the most fervent prayers of her life, pleading for wisdom to recognize God's will and a sense of direction with her writing talents.

Staring her in the face and speaking rapidly with a thick French accent was a man whom she would soon come to know as an ill-mannered and annoying yet brilliant and passionate prophet of the streets who found in every possible circumstance a preachable moment. His mission in life was to advocate for the poor and marginalized, provide work for the common laborer, and enlighten the Church and society at large about the works of mercy and social justice because the institutional Church wasn't expressing much interest in those things.

He had big ideas about forming a radical Christian movement at the service of traditional Catholic social teachings on justice and peace, something most Catholics, including Dorothy, didn't even know existed. He saw the plight of the hungry homeless begging for food, felt the cry of minorities struggling for civil rights, and heard the roar of laborers demanding just wages and the right to organize against big business. The Gospels and papal encyclicals were his "weapons" against the injustices of communism and capitalism, and his reminders to Church leaders of what Jesus was really about beneath all the guilt and rules on which they tended to focus.

Peter Maurin breathed new life into Dorothy's faith just as it was beginning to falter. As a recent Catholic whose conversion had lost her all of her friends, she was scandalized and embarrassed by the occurrences of hypocrisy in Church leadership, their courting of the rich and powerful, their disdain for the poor, and their emphasis on fear and punishment over love and compassion. As an antidote, Peter taught that we must pray constantly for the Church's leaders, not abandon them in contempt or disgust. It is the more loving, more creative thing to do and therefore the more Christ-like. If we truly love it, we must work together at making it better. We must revel in the beauty of it, not cave in to despair over its shortcomings.

Once it was decided that a newspaper would be the best way to spread all this good news, Dorothy discovered a way to bridge her two loves, the social activism of her life as a journalist in the city and the contemplative creativity of her life as a writer on Staten Island—*ora et labora* and the story of Mary and Martha rolled into one. Her prayers for a sense of direction in life were answered; her sense of purpose was re-energized and her faith restored. Right there in Dorothy's living room, without a clue as to what would come of it, the Catholic Worker was born.

Peter remained Dorothy's beloved mentor and soul friend until his death. For the last five years of his life, he was sick and often in pain, unable to speak or think clearly. He died in 1949 on the feast of St. Isidore the Farmer. Dorothy was on the road at the time and got the call at midnight. She and some friends knelt in the living room of the farmhouse where she was staying and prayed the Office of the Dead. He was laid out in the offices of the Catholic Worker at 115 Mott Street; his funeral was celebrated at Transfiguration Church, also on Mott Street; and he was buried in St. John's Cemetery in Queens.

Less than a week later, Dorothy received notice that the building on 115 Mott Street, which had housed the Catholic Worker since the late thirties, was being sold and they would have to move. That was all the proof she needed to know that Peter was still with them.

Those who sow in tears
will reap with cries of joy.
Those who go forth weeping,
carrying sacks of seed,
Will return with cries of joy,
carrying their bundled sheaves.
(Psalm 126:5–6)

Today, 115 Mott Street is a storefront selling Chinese herbal remedies and beauty supplies. I sketched it with a cup of hot coffee at hand on a bitterly cold morning when the temperature was 9 degrees.

PART II
MARY'S CANTICLE

The hungry God has filled with good things;
the rich God has sent away empty.

(Luke 1:53)

THE CATHOLIC WORKER IS BORN
COMMUNITY LIFE, POVERTY, WORKS OF MERCY

We should hide our littleness in God's greatness and stay there hidden like a little bird beneath its mother's sheltering wing.

—*Francis de Sales*

Love in action is a harsh and dreadful thing compared with love in dreams.

—*Fyodor Dostoevsky*

Peter knew he couldn't live out his radical dream alone. He was a rapidly talking, incessantly preaching head in search of a heart. He was humble enough to know that it takes teamwork to get such original ideas off the ground. Church history is filled with saintly pairs of soul friends who pooled their complementary gifts and energies into vibrant religious movements that met the needs and challenges of their day and transformed the entire Church in the process. Among the most noteworthy are Benedict and Scholastica, Francis and Clare of Assisi, Teresa of Ávila and John of the Cross, Francis de Sales and Jane de Chantal, and Vincent de Paul and Louise de Marillac.

Each of these momentous partnerships involved the founding of a religious community to perform the tasks of prayer and mercy. But

things were different in 1932, when Peter Maurin and Dorothy Day gave birth to an entirely new concept: communities of laypeople (who didn't have to be Catholic) organized to perform the works of mercy previously left to religious orders. Peter's program was centered on three main components that together would create a new heaven and a new earth right in capitalist America: the creation of houses of hospitality to address the overwhelming reality of unemployment and hunger during the Depression; Friday evening roundtable discussions open to anyone, to foster his belief that workers should become scholars and scholars workers; and the creation of worker farms, which would not only provide fresh food, but give people a sense of the dignity of labor and respect for the environment.

All of it was to be done in the context of Christian community. But unlike men and women in religious orders, Catholic Workers wouldn't have to make a lifelong commitment, nor would they live under the rule of a superior. Although the workers would not profess the traditional vows of chastity, poverty, and obedience, they would embrace the spirit of those vows, especially poverty. The abject poverty Dorothy witnessed on the Lower East Side of Manhattan, along with the simple life she lived on Staten Island, inspired in her a love for voluntary poverty and detachment from material comforts.

Such radical witness to the gospel and works of mercy not only meant being hospitable to the grimy faces of Jesus at the door, who were rarely convenient, sometimes drunk or insane, and occasionally ungrateful, but making bold statements about Catholic social values in the face of capitalism, violence, war, and greed. It meant learning to live with rats, roaches, lice, and no hot water or privacy. It meant looking for God in the margins of life, recognizing beauty in unexpected faces, and proclaiming that absolutely nothing matters in this world but love.

[It is the LORD] who keeps faith forever,
secures justice for the oppressed,
gives food to the hungry.
The LORD sets prisoners free.
The LORD protects the stranger,
sustains the orphan and widow.

(Psalm 146:6c–7, 9ab)

ON THE WRITING LIFE: THE WRITTEN WORD

We become like the things we love.

—*Francis de Sales*

Writing is an act of community. It is a part of our human association with each other. It is an expression of our love and concern for each other.

—*Dorothy Day*

From the time she was a young girl, Dorothy was a voracious reader. All her life, in letters, books, and conversations, she could liberally quote passages from the works of her favorite authors, moving easily from St. Augustine to Dickens to Tolstoy. And she didn't just stick with the classics; she stayed current with contemporary writers as well. The Russian novelists were always her favorites, however, with Dostoevsky in particular leading the pack. She found their work so theologically and spiritually enlightening that she read them over and over again throughout her life: *War and Peace*, *The Brothers Karamazov*, *Anna Karenina*, and *The Idiot*. In the latter she discovered her life motto, "The world will be saved by beauty."

Dorothy said that referring to great writers, which she did frequently in her letters and journal entries, kept her balanced. Reading them not only nurtured her love for words, it helped her discover her own style as a writer and journalist. Over the decades she wrote several spiritual memoirs (the most famous being *The Long Loneliness*) plus hundreds of articles for the *Catholic Worker* and other leading Catholic periodicals.

Her own journalistic instincts (plus being the daughter of a journalist) prompted Dorothy to write about real people in real situations, whether they were the staff at the Worker, their guests in the breadlines, or her fellow passengers on a bus ride across the country. Through them, she wrote columns that were intended to inspire her readers, not depress them, and also to educate them about the realities of life for the poor, homeless, addicted, and mentally ill—to proclaim and acclaim, not denounce or judge.

> I was all for plunging right in. After all, I had a typewriter and a kitchen table and plenty of paper and plenty to write about.
>
> I am a journalist and well trained in that, what with a father and three brothers, all of whom were journalists.

This natural talent also fed her devotion to letter writing, an art that she took most seriously. For Dorothy, like Francis de Sales before her, letter writing was a ministry of sharing sage advice and spiritual consolation. She herself estimated that she wrote a thousand letters a year (except that she didn't have to use a quill pen, as Francis did).

Francis wrote an estimated twenty thousand letters of spiritual direction in his lifetime. They are a treasure trove of advice to ordinary people on ways to find God in their everyday routines and circumstances. His writing style may seem a bit dated to us today, a little flowery and overly expressive to our modern senses, but the messages beneath the words are timeless. Francis constantly drew on science and the beauty of nature to create relevant analogies to our life in God. Everything he wrote was intended to be practical enough for the average person to gain access to spiritual truth.

When he was a newly ordained priest working as a missionary in the remotest regions of the Alps, Francis de Sales developed an inspiringly brilliant—and radical—way of reaching the hearts of as many people as possible. He printed devotional pamphlets and left them under doors and in public places. Written in French, not Latin, they gave tips on how to pray as well as lessons from the catechism. This had a direct influence on Dorothy as she began the *Catholic Worker* newspaper.

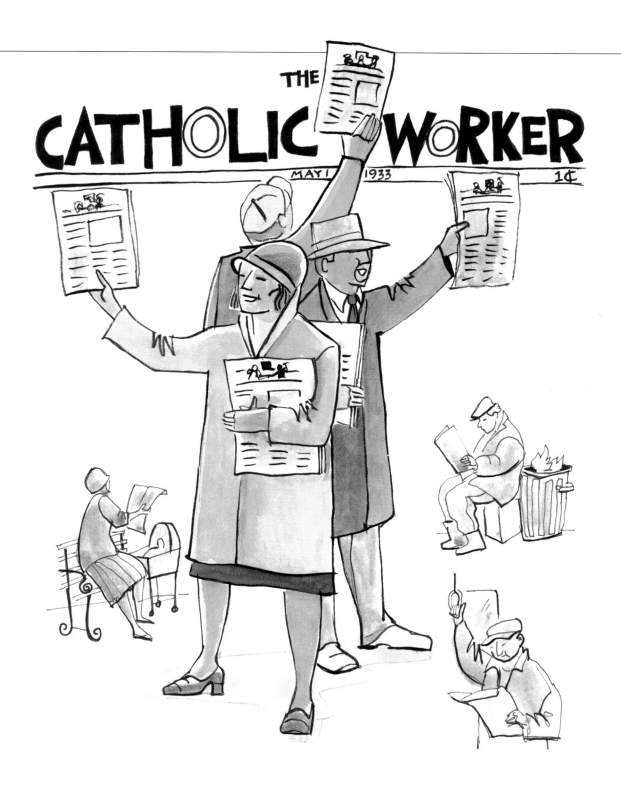

The first issue of the *Catholic Worker* newspaper came out on May 1, 1933, as an alternative to the Communist observance of May Day, which was created to celebrate workers and laborers. Twenty-five hundred copies were printed that first time. Three months later, they needed to print twenty-five thousand and within one year, one hundred fifty thousand! It cost just a penny a copy, which is still the price today.

Just a few doors down from my studio on Jasper Street, across from Sacred Heart Parish in south Camden in what used to be a vacant lot sandwiched into a row of houses, we have a most unique place for rest and meditation. Visitors enter this garden, called The Poet's Walk, through a brick archway with a wrought iron gate. In the center is an old millstone set altar-like on a column. Embedded in the millstone is a brick from James Joyce's childhood home in Dublin, a gift to Father Doyle from an Irish poet who visited the parish several years ago. It is one of the many reasons why I love living and working in Camden, with all its hidden delights.

The Poet's Walk is paved with bricks, many inscribed with the names of their benefactors' favorite writers and poets, which makes for some pretty interesting relationships. Where else could one find Shakespeare alongside Tupac Shakur and Dr. Seuss? Walking around the space you will encounter everyone from God to Walt Whitman to Flannery O'Connor and Maya Angelou. And right there, in this lovely and unique garden, amid the heartbreaking challenges of Camden city, you can take a moment or two to recall beauty and those who craft beauty from words, and God, the source of all that beauty, who in the beginning was the Word.

My heart is stirred by a noble theme,
as I sing my ode to the king.
My tongue is the pen of a nimble scribe.

(Psalm 45:2)

THE WORD AS IMAGE

The sight of beauty causes us to love it, and love for it causes us to gaze at it.

—Francis de Sales

We need to bring beauty into the midst of ugliness. It honors and glorifies God. To see such beauty from the dung heap of a slum.

—Dorothy Day

In 1934, before the *Catholic Worker* newspaper was even a year old, a young art student from Belgium named Ade Bethune (1914–2002) sent in some of her drawings for Dorothy to consider for publication. She had seen a copy of the first issues and felt they were, shall we say, "aesthetically challenged." After all, she argued, the Communist newspaper, *The Masses*, looked impressive with lots of eye-catching graphic designs. Shouldn't the *Catholic Worker* strive for the same? Dorothy loved her work and her ideas, and before long Ade Bethune's beautiful black and white ink drawings established a visual standard that survives to this day.

The look they agreed on suggested a medieval illuminated manuscript but with the clean, crisp lines of Art Deco in the modern industrial age. One of Ade's earliest assignments was to design the masthead. To reflect the audience they were trying to reach and the high rate of unemployment in the depths of the Depression, Ade depicted two laborers, one white and one black, with Christ standing between them, his hands on their shoulders. Fifty years later, in recognition of the women's and farm workers' movements, Ade turned the white man into a woman farmer with a basket of vegetables and a baby on her back.

> Ade Bethune's drawings always arrest the attention of the men for a moment. No matter how anxious they are about reaching the coffee pot there is always time to cast eyes along the wall.

Another artist classically associated with the *Catholic Worker* was Fritz Eichenberg (1900–1990), a young Jewish man who fled with his wife and baby from Germany to the United States when Hitler came to power. Once during World War I, when he was a teenager in Cologne, he fainted from malnutrition right at the rectory door of a priest who happened to be an art historian and curator. This kind man gave him food, but even more importantly, when he learned that Fritz was an artist, gave him art books and set him on the path to becoming one of the greatest print makers in modern art. Fritz would one day write the standard textbook on printmaking used by art students everywhere (including this one!). His first religious works were inspired by St. Francis of Assisi, whom he saw as an exemplar of beauty, justice, and God's mercy. Illustrating this great saint and hero was his way of thanking God for the gift of art and the kindness of strangers.

Dorothy met Fritz, who converted to Quakerism after his wife died, at Pendle Hill, a Quaker retreat center outside Philadelphia. When she discovered their mutual love for Dostoevsky, Tolstoy, and Dickens, whose works he had illustrated, she asked him to do some work for her. His first visit to the *Catholic Worker* was all the convincing he needed. By the time he died, he had done over a hundred engravings of stories from the Gospels and lives of the saints for the newspaper. He didn't care what critics thought of this particular work, if it was too "unsophisticated," because he didn't really work

for art critics—he worked for God and the often illiterate people at Worker houses, who were deeply moved by seeing Christ standing in the breadlines with them.

> One couldn't help loving Dorothy. Her laughter was something I liked to provoke. Her love of art, music, literature was passionate, a love that lifted her out of the day-by-day sacrificial and self-ordained vocation of living with the poor, the rejected, the lacerated, the untouchables.

What is so important about the work of these two artists, and all of the artists who have contributed their work over the decades, is that they didn't do it for the cultured elite. Like Peter Maurin, they felt that art must be taken off its intellectual pedestal and be accessible to common, ordinary working people. It had to be simple, clear, and inviting. It also had to honor the traditions of Christian art and symbolism, yet have a fresh, contemporary look.

Dorothy had a real soft spot for anyone engaged in the works of beauty because it is sacred work that mirrors the works of mercy. When we hunger and thirst for love, art soothes our loneliness; when we feel emotionally naked and raw, art clothes us in self-respect; when we are imprisoned by our own self-absorption and sinfulness, art frees our spirits so we can see our true needs as well as the needs of others around us. Art and beauty bring joy to the sick and depressed, and best of all, a favorite piece of art or music provides the shelter to which our roaming hearts can always come home.

In my own travels these past few years I have been blessed to encounter some wonderful instances of beauty and mercy going hand in hand, places where the Holy Spirit is clearly up to her tricks of healing enlightenment.

Since 1987, I have been a teacher at The Grunewald Guild, an interfaith art community in the Cascade Mountains that holds weeklong classes throughout the summer on a wide variety of subjects ranging from painting and fiber arts to stained-glass window making and song writing. Through art and a countless series of "Aha!" moments, seekers of all faiths and levels of ability gain new understanding of themselves as co-creators with the Holy Spirit in one of the most beautiful parts of the country.

At St. Francis de Sales School (you just knew I had to get him in here somehow!), high atop a hill in Morgantown, West Virginia, the art teacher, Nora Sheets, has her elementary school students creating amazing artwork based on themes of social justice, from feeding the hungry to banning land mines in foreign countries. The

kids do research into Catholic social teaching and famous artists, which inspires their amazingly sophisticated art. One time, they created six-foot-tall puppets with moveable parts depicting saints and heroes. Mahatma Gandhi and Martin Luther King stood alongside Mother Teresa and Mary on a hill overlooking the gorgeous Appalachian valley below. These blessed kids sketch and carve and paint and grow like weeds in wisdom and understanding of all things holy . . . and have fun while they're at it.

When the Benedictine Sisters of Erie, Pennsylvania, moved out of their inner-city monastery, they didn't abandon the people in the neighborhood. They turned their former monastery into an education facility, and even more exciting (to me), transformed an old tire store a few blocks away into an after-school arts center. Painting, drawing, dance, creative writing, and music have given the children of a challenged neighborhood new hopes and dreams in an old garage.

Father Michael Boccaccio, the pastor at St. Philip's Church in Norwalk, Connecticut, has created a new use for the old mansion on the parish property that was once the convent. He founded SPAG, St. Philip's Art Gallery. The ten bedrooms have been converted into studios occupied by artists in need of affordable workspace. Changing exhibits of paintings and sculpture are held in galleries throughout the building, with themes directly or indirectly related to peace and social justice, such as hunger or water shortages around the world.

Lastly, there's Marge Nykaza from Chicago. As a young and talented singer years ago, she opted for marriage and a family instead of a career in opera. With her kids now grown and moved on, she has created a second career for herself called Harmony, Hope, and Healing, through which homeless and addicted women are finding new ways to stay clean by singing in a choir that travels to different churches around Chicago every Sunday.

Encouraging stories such as these are happening in church venues across the country in every denomination and social milieu. People of faith everywhere are hungry for reasons to stay in the churches they love, but which are all too often dreary and unwelcoming at best. Beauty heals us because it inspires awe and wonder in the face of life's mysteries; it brings us optimism and joy, and gently reminds us that when all is said and done, all that matters is Love.

One day Dorothy asked Ade to do a drawing of St. Francis de Sales to illustrate a story about him that meant a lot to her. It seems that Francis's servant had a habit of coming home drunk at night. One time he passed out at the front door, where our saint found him, picked him up, and put him in his own bed while he sat up all night in a nearby chair and prayed for him. When the servant awoke to see St. Francis there serenely praying for him, he mended his ways and never drank again. Dorothy loved the story because of the many alcoholics who came as guests to the Catholic Worker house. She needed a beautiful yet simple reminder that everyone who knocked at the door was Christ himself, no matter what their condition or appearance, and Ade's drawing, seen in my interpretation here, did the trick.

You formed my inmost being;
you knit me in my mother's womb.
I praise you, so wonderfully you made me;
wonderful are your works!

(Psalm 139:13–14)

12 THE GARDEN STATE

The church is a garden patterned with many colors.

—*Francis de Sales*

God is our creator. God made us in His image and likeness. Therefore we are creators. He gave us a garden to till and cultivate. . . . The joy of creativeness should be ours.

—*Dorothy Day*

Ecological awareness and environmental justice are key teachings in the contemporary Catholic catechism, and once again the Catholic Worker was ahead of the curve in that regard. Peter Maurin loved to say that the Catholic Worker is not an organization, but an organism—a living, breathing, growing thing different from anything the institutional Church had ever seen. Catholic Worker farms were created as retreat houses where workers could get away from the busy city houses and find contemplative peace. On the farms and in the gardens, scholars and laborers would work side by side as equals, tilling, planting, growing, and harvesting, united in their common mission of cultivating a more just world.

Every year, scores of volunteers plant potatoes on the feast of St. Patrick.

You can't be blamed for wondering why New Jersey is called the Garden State if your only reference point is the city of Camden. If you just speed through town in terror, as many locals do, their doors locked and eyes fixed forward, you will miss the finer points, which can be seen and experienced only when you hang out for a while. Behind my studio, for example, is a small farm plot with chickens and a greenhouse teeming with thick, green life. That greenhouse is one of the reasons I chose to move here, and that urban garden is one of many that are springing up all around the city.

Flowers, fruit, vegetables, and even tilapia fish are farmed there and sometimes cooked in an outdoor oven during cooking classes for the neighborhood kids. I can watch the smoke curling out of the chimney from my studio window. To see lush greenery and vibrant color in vacant lots once strewn with dead grass and debris brings the healing promise of hope in ways that nothing else can. It offers those of us who live and work in Camden an alternative to thinking of our city as merely poor and violent, or our Church as merely sinful and scandalous. Gardens bring neighbors together in our ongoing creation story.

If you ever come to Camden to do some volunteer service work, not only will we welcome you with open arms, we will put a shovel or a paintbrush in your hands. We believe that cultivating beauty feeds the soul just as much as making sandwiches feeds the body. These things are the bare necessities of a life lived fully and well, not mere niceties. Gardens are healing places because they are living proof of God's extravagant love. They slow us down when we are too caught up in the frantic pace of life and remind us of other realities, both seen and unseen.

This rain park was created to prevent sewer backup and flooding and to bring beauty to an industrial area on a corner once dominated by an abandoned gas station.

Filipinos celebrate Misa de Gallo ("The rooster's Mass") before sunrise for nine days before Christmas. The rooster announces the coming of Christ as well as the dawn.

Throughout art history, in just about every culture and religion, gardens have been the symbolic places where God intervenes directly in human life. God walked through the Garden of Eden, enjoying what had been created. In traditional Christian art, the angel Gabriel appears to Mary in a garden and announces the good news of her pregnancy, and thus her body itself becomes a garden where the seed of the Tree of Life is planted. Jesus suffered in agony in the Garden of Gethsemane the night before he died, and rose from the dead in a garden tomb. Gardens abound in Judaism, Islam, and Buddhism as mystical places where humans are enlightened. That's true to this day, even in New Jersey.

Love and truth will meet;
justice and peace will kiss.
Truth will spring from the earth;
justice will look down from heaven.
*The L*ORD *will surely grant abundance;*
our land will yield its increase.

(Psalm 85:11–13)

THE SAINTS

Choose particular saints whose lives you can appreciate and imitate and in whose intercession you have confidence.

—*Francis de Sales*

I get so impatient sometimes that I have to go off by myself and read St. Francis de Sales' letters to calm myself.

—*Dorothy Day*

From her earliest days as a Catholic, Dorothy had an abiding love for the saints, invoking them, relying on them, quoting them, learning from them, and finding in them a genuine source of joy and encouragement. The saints were as real to her as her flesh-and-blood friends and letter correspondents. They were soul companions who inspired her to keep going when the going got tough; they were mentors who pointed out the way to holiness; they were counselors who taught her how to communicate with her own demons and shadows as well as her guests.

The saints also taught Dorothy the art of hospitality—of opening not only her home to Jesus, but her heart as well, in ways that were sometimes painfully uncomfortable. St. Elizabeth Seton, a fellow Staten Islander, used to advise that we should prepare to meet our grace every day; for Dorothy that grace was just as readily found in conversations over a cup of coffee with her guests, who weren't necessarily always sober, sane, or lemony fresh, as in her political activism on behalf of the poor and marginalized. Grace emboldened Dorothy to step out of her comfort

zones. She felt it wasn't enough merely to soothe the many social ills that plague us; we must work at preventing and changing them. It is the difference between charity and true Christian love. For example, while she was edified by St. Peter Claver, who ministered to the shiploads of slaves who survived the horrors of the middle passage, she wondered where the saints were who worked at eradicating slavery in the first place.

In all things big and small, saints were in the details. Dorothy didn't fret about bills and eviction notices; she tucked them under a statue of Joseph, who always took care of those things. She didn't sit alone in a jail cell; she turned to Paul, who gave her the courage to enter her fear and transform it into eloquence and poetry. She didn't walk by herself through the slums; she walked with Vincent de Paul and Louise de Marillac, whose love for the poorest of the poor she shared (Vincent told Louise's Daughters of Charity that their cloister was to be the streets). She didn't do dishes alone; she heard Teresa of Ávila say that God dwells in the pots and pans. She didn't sweep the floor by herself; Martin de

Porres lent a hand. She didn't shun the repulsive; she embraced them with Francis of Assisi, who kissed a leper and discovered the transforming face of God. (In imitation, she once kissed a woman hideously deformed by face cancer.)

Dorothy entertained her countless guests with Mary and Martha, who always had room for one particularly important guest in their home in Bethany. She loved opera and art, as did Alphonsus Liguori, who adored the Naples Opera and sometimes painted his homilies. She farmed and gardened with Isidore, who stopped for prayer breaks in the midst of labor. She visited the dying with Brigid of Ireland, who used straw from the floor to weave a cross as she told the story of Jesus to a dying Druid king. She buried the dead with Catherine of Siena, who provided proper Christian burials for plague victims who died alone on the streets and told the Avignon pope to go back to Rome where he belonged. Like Anthony of Padua, she outspokenly despised clericalism; and like Joan of Arc, she had the courage to follow her conscience and speak truth to power and authority.

Of all the saints, however, Dorothy's lifelong favorites were Teresa of Ávila, for whom she named her daughter Tamar Teresa, and Thérèse of Lisieux, about whom she wrote a spiritual biography. She fell in love with Teresa of Ávila, one of the first saints she read about, in her early days as a Catholic, because of her down-to-earth, humorous practicality mixed with a contemplative, mystical spirit. Teresa used to pray to be spared from sour-faced saints, and grumbled that life was a night spent in a messy inn. Both remarks spoke to the realities of daily life in community.

Dorothy wasn't initially impressed with Thérèse the Little Flower, finding her autobiography, *Story of a Soul*, to be little more than pious pap. But eventually, Thérèse captivated Dorothy and an endless legion of devotees in the twentieth century with her spirituality of "The Little Way," which, with its emphasis on the ordinary little virtues, is so practical and down to earth. No matter how unmemorable the little things we do—cooking, cleaning, visiting, going to work, getting kids ready for school, sitting in traffic—they are opportunities to practice kindness and patience. Little steps lead to great love; the least among us are the greatest in God's eyes. Thérèse's Little Way was the foundation on which the Catholic Worker was built and continues to thrive.

As for the Francis de Sales "six degrees of separation" moment you've been waiting for, he had a huge influence on Thérèse. Not only did her parents love the *Introduction to the Devout Life*, her aunt and her sister Léonie were both Visitandine nuns. High up in the Basilica of St. Thérèse in Lisieux is a row of stained-glass windows depicting her favorite saints. Francis is there alongside Joan of Arc, Cecilia, John Vianney, and Teresa of Ávila.

Which brings us to Mother Teresa of Calcutta, who also based her heroic work on the Little Way. She instructed her sisters, the Missionaries of Charity, not to speak about Jesus to their guests, but rather to *be* Jesus. They first met in India, where Mother Teresa invited Dorothy to give an impromptu talk to the novices. Dorothy spoke to them about Gandhi and the lessons she learned from him about non-violent resistance. When she finished, Mother Teresa pinned a profession cross on her blouse and pronounced her "one of us." It was the beginning of a loving, lifelong friendship. Years later, when Mother Teresa went to New York, she visited Dorothy at the Catholic Worker.

Dorothy Day was a mystic who discovered God in the details of nature; a journalist with unbounded curiosity and the need to get to the bottom of things; a mother whose heart brimmed with joy at the little achievements of her children and ached with sorrow at their big losses (and the occasional "Maybe I could have done that better"); a lay minister who loved praying with people and hearing their stories; and a writer who could magically weave all these things together into a thing of beauty from a place too deep for words. Her very life was a revelation of God's abundant generosity to the rest of us. Sounds pretty saintly to me!

Time and again in over fifty years' worth of journal entries, letters, articles, and speeches, Dorothy quoted St. John of the Cross. It is a sweet lesson for all of us sinners stumbling on our way to sanctity: "Where there is no love, put love, and there you will draw out love."

St. Francis de Sales had a great love for the saints who preceded him. He considered them not merely his spiritual ancestors, but his teachers of the faith. St. Paul inspired him with missionary zeal and the art of letter writing, Augustine with his thirst for beauty and spiritual transformation, Blessed Teresa (as he called Teresa of Ávila) with her mystical practicality. He loved Ignatius and so chose Jesuits as his personal spiritual directors. Charles Borromeo's gentle and pastoral manner inspired his approach to being a bishop, and his own patron, Francis of Assisi, filled him with love for the poor and holy simplicity.

Many of the saints during and after his time considered him a key inspiration in their own spiritual development. Vincent de Paul was his dear friend and Louise de Marillac one of his spiritual directees; Alphonsus Liguori was inspired by his love of beauty and culture; John de la Salle made Francis's motto, "Live Jesus," the motto of the Christian Brothers; Elizabeth Seton read the *Introduction to the Devout Life* on her knees every night; John Neumann spent his last mark on a full set of Francis's books before leaving home in Bohemia for America; Katharine Drexel named her first school St. Francis after de Sales, not Assisi; and Blessed Pope John XXIII considered Charles Borromeo and Francis de Sales his spiritual mentors.

In the presence of angels I sing to you.
(Psalm 138:1c, New Jerusalem Bible)

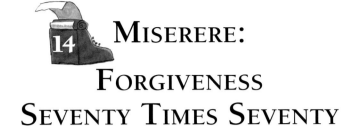

MISERERE:
FORGIVENESS
SEVENTY TIMES SEVENTY

My dealings with people are always honest, simple, and in good faith. I cannot put on a double face, and I hate duplicity with a mortal hatred.

—Francis de Sales

No matter how corrupt the Church may become, it carries within itself the seeds of its own regeneration. To read the lives of the saints has always helped me.

—Dorothy Day

St. Francis de Sales was a bishop who was renowned and loved throughout France because he said and wrote things like the quote above. Never a climber, he turned down the chance to become Cardinal Archbishop of Paris, declining to desert his "poor wife" Geneva, for a richer one, Paris. While he had great respect for his role as bishop, especially in the still tumultuous, often exhilarating, times of Catholic reform following the Council of Trent, he never let it go to his head or used it as a means for his own personal advancement. The primary teacher of his diocese, he was never afraid to be the primary student as well, to learn from the poor widows and village folk who loved him and looked to him for inspiration. In Salesian spirituality, humility is the greatest of all the little virtues because it leads to reconciliation. It is like sunshine that melts a frozen heart.

Francis was both a canon and civil lawyer but his main priority as bishop was not to teach his flock about rules, regulations, and codes of canon law, but rather to teach them that no matter what they do or who they are, they are loved by God. He also set out to teach them how to return God's love; how to lead a devout life while living fully in the world; how to live with stress by praying in practical, doable ways and discover God's will for their lives. He even addressed the readers of his books as *Philothea* and *Theotimus*, or "lovers of God." He believed that when Jesus said, "Feed my sheep," he didn't mean their heads; he meant their hearts.

Now here's the best part, the most human part. This holy man, so renowned for his gentle and courteous demeanor, so revered for the inner serenity that seemed to make him glow, was by nature a very angry, temperamental guy! He was, he insisted, as human as could possibly be, and thus worked extra hard at overpowering his weaknesses so they would not have power over him. We must practice gentleness and patience

Poor widows and village folk are full of goodness & devotion while we Bishops — who are called to the Church's heights — are cold & unfeeling. Is there no sunshine to melt the chilliness of my Heart?

St. Francis De Sales

with ourselves first, he taught, before we can expect to do it with others.

Dorothy had similar inclinations toward anger and judgment, and prayed continually for the strength and wisdom to overcome them. She never failed to beg people's forgiveness when they were the victims of her sharp tongue or rash judgments. As she said time and again, the toughest part of being Christian, the harshest and most dreadful side of loving Jesus, is this demand that we be reconciled and forgive our enemies seventy times seven. Hardest of all, Jesus said, when those enemies come from within your very household.

When the wild and crazy sixties arrived in a burst of sexual freedom and exploration, Dorothy prayed with extra fervor not to judge the youth too harshly, especially those who lived at the Catholic Worker. She recalled all too well her own young adulthood, when she was "intoxicated by the freedom of it all." She humbly admitted to having committed all the same sins save drug abuse that plague modern youth. But she felt particularly blessed, she said, to have prayed a lifetime of *Memorares* and Acts of Contrition since those more carefree days.

The abortion Dorothy had had as a young woman was her biggest regret in life. But, she always said, where sin abounds, grace abounds doubly—and that grace urged her forward to bigger, better things than guilt and self-hatred. Once she forgave herself and stopped judging herself, she could do the same for others. It was at the very heart of her conversion to Catholicism, this belief that we are made in the image and likeness of God and are therefore beautiful in God's sight—no matter who we are or what mistakes we make. Penance and reconciliation are, in this light, wondrous gifts that open our eyes to new visions of beauty.

It was far more difficult for her to forgive the weaknesses of some Church leaders, who sometimes seemed to be her greatest enemies within this Church household she so dearly loved. It was easier for her to locate Jesus in the homeless at her door, no matter how needy or repugnant, than in the faces of those who abused their own power and authority. She prayed continually for the strength to push aside her judgments and flashes of anger, and dwell instead on the more likeable characteristics of disagreeable people— no matter how deep she had to scratch.

As a convert, I never expected much of the bishops. In all history popes and bishops and father abbots seem to have been blind and power hungry and greedy. I never expected leadership from them. It is the saints who keep appearing all through history, who keep things going. What I do expect is the bread of life and down through the ages that there is that continuity.

From her first days as a Catholic, people frequently asked Dorothy how she could stay entangled in a church so out of touch with ordinary people, so righteous and power hungry. In response, she quoted the theologian Romano Guardini (a mentor of Pope Benedict XVI), who once said, "The Church is the cross on which Christ was crucified, and Christ cannot be separated from his cross." She believed that true reform starts with the village folk, including the saints, through prayer, sacrifice, and penance; that human hearts are set free by grace and the tender mercy of Jesus and shouldn't be constrained by fear, anger, or judgment. In fixing her heart on Jesus and the sacraments, and not fixating on the shortcomings of an all-too-human hierarchy, Dorothy was never in danger of losing her faith. Having it challenged and tested, yes; but losing it, never.

Restore my joy in your salvation;
sustain in me a willing spirit.
I will teach the wicked your ways,
that sinners may return to you.

(Psalm 51:14–15)

PEACE, POPES, AND PROTESTS

Nothing should have the power to take away our peace; even if everything goes wrong and turns topsy-turvy, it shouldn't let it worry me, for what's the whole world put together compared with a peaceful heart?

—*Francis de Sales*

We are not asking God to deliver us from enemies, but from the fear of them. Love casts out all fear, but we have to get over the fear in order to get close enough to love them.

—*Dorothy Day*

In the medieval world in the crusading throes of anti-Muslim fear and animosity, St. Francis of Assisi instructed the friars that if they should ever happen upon the pages of the Qur'an, they should reverently place them on the altar, not desecrate them, because they were sacred. He knew that the pen is mightier than the sword, and is credited with composing the magnificent "Peace Prayer," one of the most cherished prayers in Church history. All of this explains why he was one of Dorothy's favorite saints and role models—he created beauty as an alternative to fear.

Growing up in the waning days of the Reformation, Francis de Sales witnessed the same bitter hatred and violence that Francis of Assisi did—only now it was within the Christian family between Catholics and Protestants, whose only common bond was their mutual disdain for Jews and Muslims. Memories of violence against people and the destruction of church property, all in the name of Jesus, didn't fit with his notion of Christianity. So when he became Bishop of Geneva but could not live in the city forbidden

to Catholics, he sneaked in on three occasions to meet secretly with the head of the Calvinist Church. Francis felt that respectful dialogue, not angry rhetoric, was the only way to maintain peace and overcome fear of "the other" or fear of what is different from us.

Dorothy's uncompromising and courageous views on peace, non-violence, and conscientious objection didn't please all the people of her time either. Each decade of twentieth-century history gave reasons for Catholic Workers to practice what they preached about war and peace. In the thirties it was the Spanish Civil War; in the forties, World War II, when the number of Catholic Worker houses plummeted; in the fifties, the Korean and Cold Wars; in the sixties, civil rights; and in the early seventies, Vietnam. Dorothy challenged the power structures of Church and government to stop planting the seeds of fear in people's hearts and to promote love and tolerance instead.

Dorothy's approach to public protests was the same as her columns in the *Catholic Worker* newspaper: outspoken, yes, but not overly

In April of 1963, Dorothy and fifty women from various backgrounds and denominations who called themselves "Mothers for Peace" made a pilgrimage to Rome to express their gratitude and admiration to Pope John XXIII for his encyclical Pacem in Terris, *or "Peace on Earth," which condemned the nuclear arms race. She also applauded his enthusiastic inclusion of the laity into the lifeblood of the Church and his loving devotion to the poor and outcast.*

negative, judgmental, or offensive. Like her heroes Mahatma Gandhi and Martin Luther King, she knew we can't build bridges of understanding and mutual respect with angry vitriol. She even instructed protesters representing the Catholic Worker to scrawl passages from scripture and Church teachings on their placards. Being jailed for acts of civil disobedience was a routine part of life at Catholic Worker houses.

Pope John's motto was "Obedience and Peace." He who had grown up a peasant and witnessed firsthand the horrors of two world wars and the Holocaust was clearly making his priorities known in choosing peace as the theme of his papacy, and Dorothy loved him for it. He felt that world peace begins at home from the ground up through the conscientious efforts of the faithful, which was Dorothy's thought from the beginning days of the Catholic Worker. "Obedience" for both Pope John and Dorothy meant obedience to Jesus and his teachings, especially that one about "doing unto others."

Good Pope John died just one month after the group's visit. As the American war in Vietnam continued to escalate, his successor, Pope Paul VI, spoke at the United Nations, where he famously proclaimed, "No more war!" Another line of his, "If you want peace, work for justice," was made famous on placards at every peace demonstration attended by the Catholic Worker. It soon appeared on bumper stickers and buttons across the country as people began to see the links between poverty and violence. The presence of Jesus in the tabernacle burst forth as the Jesus of the Gospels—a radical lover of the oppressed.

Dorothy returned to Rome two more times. In 1965, she and an international group of women held a ten-day hunger fast for peace to draw attention to the Council's deliberations on peace and war. She gave an interview on Vatican Radio and distributed to every bishop and cardinal copies of the *Catholic Worker* newspaper, which featured nuclear disarmament and conscientious objection. It may have changed their thinking. In 1967, she made a third trip to attend the International Congress of the Laity, where she was one of two Americans chosen to receive Communion directly from Pope Paul VI.

Dorothy turned down honorary degrees from nineteen (or so) Catholic universities that maintained ROTC programs or had ties to the defense industry. (In one stretch of time she

turned down Fordham, Holy Cross, Boston College, St. John's, and LaSalle—or, as she put it, three Jesuits, one Benedictine, and one Christian Brother.) She was investigated and bugged—in more ways than one—by the FBI and watched closely by the New York chancery. She endured nasty letters from readers of the newspaper and jeers from people on the street accusing her of being pro-Communist or anti-Catholic. But through it all, she maintained her inner peace, knowing it was love for Church and country that compelled her to challenge them.

World peace begins at home, and peace at home begins with you. Find the little ways in which you can nurture inner peace. Fast from TV shows that are violent or disturbing; cut back on twenty-four-hour cable news feeds; limit your texting and social networking. All of these things, while not bad or harmful in and of themselves, fill us with false needs and fears, and keep us in constant multi-tasking activity not conducive to inner peace. Instead, learn to be still and savor the quiet.

Some rely on chariots, others on horses,
but we on the name of the LORD our God.
They collapse and fall,
but we stand strong and firm.

(Psalm 20:8–9)

16 LOVE AND KINDNESS

We must do all through love and nothing by force.

—Francis de Sales

If we could only learn that the only important thing is love, and that we will be judged on love—to keep on loving, and showing that love, and expressing that love, over and over, whether we feel it or not. . . . Not to do anything but love, love, love.

—Dorothy Day

Forster + Nanette House, S.I.

St. Francis de Sales often referred to Calvary as the great school of love. It is through the suffering and struggles of life that we are blessed with our biggest lessons and deepest transformations. We learn to love, he used to say, by loving. It is a lifelong process of unclenching our tight fists and keeping our hearts open to reconciliation and renewal. Dramatic heroism or saintliness are neither asked of us nor expected. God knows how little we are, how weak and uncourageous, and always offers a helping hand by way of little opportunities to practice kindness and patience—to find the grace and beauty that knock at our door right alongside the pain and ugliness.

No story of Dorothy Day's life and legacy, no examples of her heroic sanctity or her many groundbreaking achievements, inspires me as much as this one from 1959. When Forster Batterham's life partner, Nanette, with whom he had taken up after his breakup with Dorothy, was stricken with cancer, he asked Dorothy to provide them with a place to live. Not only did she lend them a cottage on Staten Island, she frequently visited Nanette and sat with her, holding her hand, changing her bandages, and calming her fears.

She wouldn't have had it any other way, actually, because by that point in her life, Dorothy had truly put on Christ, filled her heart and soul with Christ, had become Christ. She had long ago let go of her futile hopes of keeping Forster in her life and courageously re-invented herself following their breakup. Jesus and pure love had given her the courage to do it. In the words attributed to her beloved St. Teresa of Ávila:

> Christ has no body now but yours; no hands, no feet on earth but yours. Yours are the eyes through which he looks compassionately on this world. . . . . Christ has no body now on earth but yours.

Nanette, who was fifteen younger than Forster, said that when she recovered from cancer (which she never did) she wanted to sell everything she had and be just like Dorothy, who had shown her Jesus. She was baptized the night before she died. For her part, Dorothy had discovered her true self through the harsher side of love, with its demands for reconciliation and that we rise above our more basic inclinations to stay mired in fear, jealousy, vengeance, or regret. She saw Nanette not as her rival, but rather as another face of Jesus, just like the countless legions she had welcomed at her door. What better way to show her love for the two great loves of her life: Jesus, to whom she had ultimately given her life, and Forster, who had given so much life to her, especially that of Tamar, their daughter?

Dorothy and Forster became loving friends again in their last years and spoke daily on the phone.

When I think of you upon my bed,
through the night watches I will recall
That you indeed are my help,
and in the shadow of your wings I shout for joy.
My soul clings fast to you.

(Psalm 63:7–9a)

Part III
Simeon's Canticle

My eyes have seen your salvation,
    which you have prepared in sight of all the peoples,
a light for revelation to the Gentiles.

(Luke 2:30–32a)

17 PRACTICING THE PRESENCE OF GOD

May God live in my heart for that is what it was made for.
—Francis de Sales

We must practice the presence of God. He is with us in our kitchens, at our tables, on our bread lines, with our visitors, on our farms.
—Dorothy Day

St. Jane de Chantal once asked St. Francis what was the longest amount of time he could go without thinking of God, and he replied fifteen minutes. He told her that he loved being alone because God felt very close to him at those times, that he could feel God's presence more in the quiet than in the busyness of work or when he had to speak. Even when he was in the presence of royalty, as he sometimes was at the French court in Paris, he didn't change his demeanor because, as he said, he was always in the presence of even greater majesty. No matter who his companion or what the circumstance, God was there as well, making him calm and peaceful. Being mindful of God's presence gave him power over his natural inclination to anger rather than giving his anger power over him.

This outlook is called the practice of the Presence of God, and Dorothy knew it well. It was her greatest tool in maintaining calm in the face of everything from finding a roach in her cereal one bright morning, to annoying interruptions from staff and guests, to the threats of being closed down for unpaid bills or violations of building codes. Whether confronted with minor inconveniences or major setbacks, Dorothy never lost her serenity. And the problems, big or small, never stopped coming. She admitted there were occasions when she never wanted to see another Catholic Worker house again, or live with difficult people in community.

Fifty years' worth of journal entries and letters show that Dorothy never missed an opportunity to pay full attention to life: her early years picking up seashells on the beach with Forster or writing beautifully vivid descriptions of Raritan Bay and the beachcombers who were her neighbors; motherhood and grandchildren; protests and

jail time; the thousands upon thousands of poor and hungry people lining up at her door over the decades to enjoy her hospitality; traveling across the country by bus to the point of exhaustion; the physical demands of arthritis and illness; and finally, her last years of confinement in Mary House, where "the early morning sun gilds the upper floors of the building across the street, creeping from the grey one to the red brick one," was all she needed for an early morning awareness of the presence of God.

Several of Dorothy's favorite methods for maintaining a centered awareness of God were taking walks around New York, retreating to the country, or knitting and weaving. She knitted on buses and trains, sitting by the fire at the various retreat houses, or during the Friday night discussions. She also kept a loom in imitation of her idol, Mahatma Gandhi. My weaver friends tell me that getting started is the complicated part, but well worth the effort, as Dorothy points out:

Setting up the loom is the hard thing. . . . What it does too is restore the sacramental aspect of things. One gets a feeling and a knowledge of God's creation, and becomes co-creator, in fashioning wool from fleece and towels from hemp and flax and to plant a bed of flax is to see a most heavenly blue mass of flowers.

Scenes outside my windows

The best way I know to be aware of God's presence is through creative activity of any kind. When I first moved to Camden, my favorite morning meditations were drawing the views outside my windows, and then eventually painting them. It not only focused me on the present moment, but trained my eyes to locate realities of beauty that had never before occurred to me. Once my painter's eyes were opened wide, I began to discover a new heaven and a new Camden, and I haven't looked back yet.

It is essential to find that one thing that works for you and puts you in a place of inner peace. Journal, garden, paint, walk on the beach, draw, sing, dance, chop vegetables and make soup, bake bread, listen to music, carve a piece of wood; or, if none of these interest you, get up fifteen minutes earlier than you'd like, put on the coffee, sit quietly in your favorite chair and simply pay attention to God, who you will see has already been up for hours paying attention to you.

The heavens declare the glory of God;
  the sky proclaims its builder's craft.
One day to the next conveys that message;
  one night to the next imparts that knowledge.
                                    (Psalm 19:2–3)

18 Beauty and Music

My father loved fine music. He had quite a record collection of classical symphonies and opera, and I often wish he were still here to tell me about it. Growing up, we kids just wrote it off as "Dad's music," something to be endured until earphones were invented. The hospital bed in which he spent his last month was in the very spot in our living room where he used to sit in his rocking chair, eyes closed and earphones in place, and go into another zone of prayerful serenity with Mozart or Strauss, his favorite composers. It was how he relaxed after a busy day at work or on a Sunday afternoon. It is one of my fondest memories of him.

One day shortly before he died, he asked my brother to find an aria he always loved from his vast collection and play it on the stereo for him. It was "Song to the Moon" from Dvořák's opera *Rusalka*. He lay there smiling faintly, eyes closed, just as he always had over the years. Through the bittersweet end of his days, music continued to be the healing gift it had been all his life. I still wonder why that particular aria at that particular time. What did it really mean to him? Did he even know himself? Like any of our encounters with beauty, I am sure he could not have put it into words even if he did know.

All her life, Dorothy had the same passion for music. *La Bohème*, she once said, haunted her youth. Every Saturday that she was home in New York, she listened to the broadcasts of the Metropolitan Opera (*Live at the Met*) on her radio. Wagner's operas were her favorite of all. She once remarked that in her next life she wanted to be a heroine from a Wagnerian opera. (Can't you see her with blonde pigtails and a Viking helmet?) On occasion she would invite others to sit with her and listen to a symphony. She cared for sick staffers by tucking them into bed with a good book and the perfect music in the background. Once, she even paid for the voice lessons of a particularly gifted staffer.

Music was her greatest recreation and favorite refuge from the storms and vicissitudes of life at the Catholic Worker, with its constant commotion and endless interruptions. Dorothy was able to face one particularly busy afternoon peacefully because she had given her entire morning over to opera. It was these meditative encounters with beauty that not only helped her to stay centered on the contemplative peace within herself, but also bestowed on her the necessary grace to recall beauty and then seek it beneath the rough surfaces of annoying staff and grimy guests.

But music wasn't her only source of beauty. In a 1977 journal entry, Dorothy wrote:

> One must search for beauty in the slums. . . . So, searching one finds it in the city, the suffering faces of the poor, . . . in the little trees struggling to survive, in pigeons on the roof across the street, on the rays of sun thru [sic] my window. By craning my neck I can glimpse the deep blue sky on sunny days.

Whenever she could, Dorothy loved to retreat to the various farms and retreat houses owned by the Catholic Worker over the years, or to walk the beach on her beloved Staten Island. The walls of her beach cottage were decorated with the vacated shells of horseshoe crabs and twisted branches of driftwood she found on her walks. On days when she felt trapped in the Bowery, she would walk the neighborhood and really see that gray and dismal corner of the world with a mystic's (and writer's) finely honed skills of observation. These small delights were signs and sacraments, giving Dorothy glimpses of the Resurrection and revealing the hidden beauty that comes with misery.

St. Francis de Sales believed that we pray best before beauty because it places us in the presence of the Source of all beauty. Plus, as scientists now tell us, it lowers our blood pressure! With beauty come hope, healing, and courage to face the storms. It forces us to see and hear with our hearts, where all people, even the most annoying and repulsive, somehow take on new dignity and light. As Dorothy used to paraphrase Teresa of Ávila, "The real measure of our love for God is the measure of love we have for the most repugnant human being we know."

> Give thanks to the LORD on the harp;
> on the ten-stringed lyre offer praise.
> Sing to God a new song;
> skillfully play with joyful chant.
>
> (Psalm 33:2–3)

Shortly after I moved to Immaculate Conception Cathedral parish in Camden, one of the homeless people who frequent our kitchen door approached me in the parking lot as I was coming home one afternoon. He asked, "Are you that artist we heard moved in here?" When I told him that indeed I was, he replied, "That's cool—we need more art around here." He's on to something, this prophetic man of the streets, because we all need more art around here, rich or poor, wherever our "here" might happen to be, whether a shelter for the homeless or a deathbed in the home. And when my time comes to leave "here," I hope and pray that beauty leads the way as it did for my father and Dorothy before me.

My heart is steadfast, God,
    my heart is steadfast.
    I will sing and chant praise.
Awake, my soul;
    awake, lyre and harp!
    I will wake the dawn.

(Psalm 57:8–9)

19

AGED BEAUTY

I keep feeling my heart to find out if advancing age is making me mean; but I find it quite the other way around—age frees me from all care and detaches my whole heart and soul from every sort of stinginess.

—*Francis de Sales*

If God wills the work to go on, it will continue. If it should take a different form, it will change, and if our task is done, it will end.

—*Dorothy Day*

Not everyone can boast of a grandmother who was able to squeeze in some jail time between baking birthday cakes and knitting sweaters. But Dorothy Day's nine grandchildren and thirteen great-grandchildren can. Family time grew increasingly important to Dorothy as she grew older, and she relished every opportunity to be with them. She was greatly disturbed that none of them practiced their Catholic faith (sound familiar?), and despite her occasional complaints that their rock-and-roll music was too loud, their skirts too short, or their parents too lenient, she loved simply being with them, especially as her travels grew less frequent.

> Do forgive this awful typing. But my hands are rheumatic and cooking and washing don't help much. My feet, too. Otherwise, I am enjoying so much being with the children.

In addition, she had many physical ailments and troubles, the most serious being arthritis and a heart condition that drastically slowed

her down. She wrote about her struggle to keep depression from getting the best of her in dark nights of the soul. But, as always, little perks and big graces came with the emotional and physical turmoil. She received personal eightieth birthday greetings from Pope Paul VI in a letter hand delivered to Maryhouse by Cardinal Terence Cooke, and another from Mother Teresa, which she cherished as one of her greatest honors. She received the Laetare Medal from Notre Dame and was invited to give her last public talk at the Eucharistic Congress in Philadelphia in 1976, where she was greeted by a thunderous ovation.

> I'm sleeping and writing a few letters and refusing to see people. They come up anyway. And then I have to make an appearance just to stop rumors I'm on my last legs. Seventy-five seems a terrific age.

Dorothy also savored the memories of her youth, sharing with her closest friends and confidants her stories of Eugene O'Neill and the other famed writers she knew so well. Fear of being perceived as a name-dropper ultimately prevented her from sharing her personal reminiscences in a book, but she did think about writing a memoir without the spiritual focus of *The Long Loneliness*.

And beauty remained her constant companion. She still derived great joy from reading and listening to symphonies and opera, and from watching films and plays on television. When she was no longer able to take her long walks around the city, she was content with the little moments of beauty she could see from her room at Maryhouse, where she spent her last years. Simple things like children playing across the street, pigeons lined up on the rooftops, flowers on her fire escape in the morning sun, all caught her mystic's eye just as small gestures of kindness touched her heart.

Forced to slow down and free of the need to work or prove ourselves anymore, there is time to honor the place of memory and history in our personal stories. Our needs change drastically as we grow in wisdom and understanding even as our bodies don't always cooperate. It is, or can be, a freeing-up time as we let go of all the things— material, physical, emotional, psychological, spiritual—that were once so important to us. Priorities shift, attachments diminish, we enter with perhaps a wobblier step into the presence of God, and rediscover ourselves all over again.

People frequently asked Dorothy if she worried about the future of the Catholic Worker after she was gone. She was way beyond worrying about anything by then, having let go of those concerns long before. It was God's work, not hers, and it wouldn't end before God's good time. She was free to go in peace, for she had loved and served the Lord.

NIGHT HOLDS NO TERRORS FOR ME SLEEPING UNDER
GOD'S WINGS.

As St. Francis de Sales lay dying, someone asked him what were the three most important virtues in life. Francis replied, "Humility, humility, humility." He taught that all of the other virtues that we struggle to practice fall into place when we practice humility first. True humility means coming to accept and embrace the circumstances of life through total abandonment to and utter reliance on God. It means accepting our lowliness and limitations and still being cheerful in the midst of it all. Truly humble people never look down on anyone, because they don't look down on themselves.

Our years end like a sigh.
Seventy is the sum of our years,
  or eighty if we are strong;
Most of them are sorrow and toil;
  they pass quickly, we are all but gone.
Teach us to count our days aright,
  that we may gain wisdom of heart.
Make us glad as many days as you have humbled us,
  for as many years as we have seen trouble.
  Prosper the work of our hands!
  Prosper the work of our hands!

(Psalm 90:9b–10, 12, 15, 17b)

THE CHURCH
EVER ANCIENT, EVER NEW

20

*I am expecting a great storm but am very cheerful all the same.
I am putting my trust in God's providence. And this certain hope
fills me with great joy.*

—Francis de Sales

*Heaven is within you. The kingdom is here and now. So joy
and suffering go together, pleasure and pain, work and rest, the
rhythm of life, day succeeding the night, spring following winter,
life and death and life again, world without end.*

—Dorothy Day

I met a priest who told me that as a seminarian in the sixties, he had to do service work at the Catholic Worker in New York. He said he learned more theology from Dorothy Day than he did in four years' worth of classes at the seminary. It's because his heart and senses were being fed, not just his head. He was living Jesus, not merely learning dogma. Just think how much richer the Church would be if the number of theology and philosophy requirements in seminary education were reduced and replaced with classes on the incredible legacy of beauty throughout the history of the Church: art history to encourage a thirst for sacred design and love for the flesh, not fear of it; music to foster inner harmony and meditation; poetry to nurture the use of eloquent words; drama to enhance preaching and liturgical presence.

Even though I was blessed with twelve years of good Catholic education, my best teachers of the faith were my parents, each of whom deeply loved the Church but who set two very different examples. My father was well informed and well read. He stayed current on the ever-changing goings-on of the Church through *Commonweal*, *America*, and the *National Catholic Reporter*. He had a wonderfully irreverent (and cynical) sense of humor about certain Church leaders and events and was not afraid to question or criticize authority. Meanwhile, my mother was a novena- and rosary-loving Catholic Daughter who never got on the el in downtown Philly without stopping at St. John's Church on Thirteenth Street for a visit. Questioning Holy Mother Church was not a consideration. Welcome to my one, true, holy, sometimes schizophrenically apostolic

Church. It is, I think, the faith of many of us in this post-conciliar, post-modern, crisis-ridden, ever-changing "shut the windows again" Church of ours. Catholicism has never been a religion for wimps, and is certainly not these days.

Dorothy Day has come to represent for me in a most prophetic way the coming together of my father's Church of Spirit-driven change and my mother's Church of reverence for tradition. Dorothy wove together the two religious cultures in which we in the modern Church struggle to move and breathe at ease, and she was able to pull it off because of her undying thirst for beauty, ever ancient, ever new. It inspired her, motivated her, comforted her, and saved her from despair. It can do the same for all people who seek common ground in a climate of such deep division.

The beauty of Dorothy's life is the way she welcomed with such astonishing graciousness the various, and often conflicting, currents and threads of Roman Catholic Christianity in the modern world. She remained to her last days a passionate lover and loyal follower of the Church with a vast knowledge of its spiritual traditions and stories. She was probably more familiar with papal encyclicals than most popes, and yet Jesus and the Gospels always took precedence over the words of mere and fallible mortals. She was as traditionally disciplined in her private life of prayer and devotion as she was radical in her theology of social justice. In short, she mastered the art of living in that seamless place of creative tension between action and contemplation, between old and new, between life in the pews and life on the streets. It is in such creative tension that beauty is born.

Baptized and formed in the "old-time religion," Dorothy maintained a deep and abiding reverence for rosaries, the saints, yearly retreats, Benediction, sacraments, and the spiritual authority of priests and bishops. She meditated every morning and prayed the Liturgy of the Hours every day and the rosary every evening. She was a daily communicant and a Third Order Benedictine who contemplated truth and beauty while praying before the Blessed Sacrament. "I'm just an old conservative," she'd say when asked about women's ordination or birth control, yet she was not afraid to challenge bishops to practice what they should have been preaching, even traveling to Rome to do so.

None of these things were at odds with other sides of her personal spirituality. Beginning in 1933, long before anyone else (including most bishops) was thinking of these things, and long before Vatican II, Dorothy, a laywoman yet, actually read the Gospels and discovered in them the root and source of Catholic social teaching. They revealed to her a Jesus alive and well outside of the monstrance and in the faces of broken, downtrodden, insane, addicted, and sinful humanity. These were his sheep, whom he commanded her to shepherd. A new kind of beauty opened up before her eyes when she came to see the works of mercy, peace, and justice as an entryway into the heart of Christ, a way that incorporated a whole community of hearts: the other workers with whom she labored side by side and the endless stream of hungry strangers who, decade upon decade, knocked at her door for food, shelter, and communion over a cup of coffee.

My parents and Dorothy have taught me that a well-integrated life is a creative and balanced life. Back in the day, *In medio stat virtus* ("In the middle lies virtue") was really another way of saying that a "both/and" frame of mind is more enlightening than an "either/or" one. Open minds and humble hearts welcome the many nuances of gray and wide spectrums of color that just aren't allowed in a black-and-white world. When seekers of beauty remain stuck in the past, they can't live fully in the present or dream of the future.

My soul rests in God alone,
from whom comes my salvation.
God alone is my rock and salvation,
my secure height; I shall never fall.
(Psalm 62:2–3)

21 DEATH AND FUNERAL

Everything done for love is love, and work is love when we accept it for love of God, and so is death itself.

—Francis de Sales

It all happened while we sat there talking, and it is still going on.

—Dorothy Day

There were eighty Catholic Worker houses across the United States at the time of Dorothy Day's death.

On the day of her funeral, a sign was posted on the front door of Maryhouse announcing that it would be closed for the day due to a death in the family. Hundreds of people gathered on the street, including staffers past and present as well as regular longtime guests, and processed with the casket to Nativity Church around the corner where the funeral Mass was celebrated. Forster Batterham and Tamar led the procession.

In keeping with the Little Way, the church was filled with the people of the streets, the regular guests of the Catholic Worker houses. One of them stretched out in the back pew for a nap during Communion and another, visibly moved, kissed Dorothy's body and lamented, "She loved us, she listened to us, she loved us."

The priest who led the graveside prayers at Resurrection Cemetery on Staten Island noted that in the middle of the service, three greyhound dogs appeared out of nowhere. The Hound of Heaven who had haunted Dorothy all her life had come to lead her home.

When can I go and see the face of God?
(Psalm 42:3b)

I lived for my art, I lived for love,
I never did harm to a living soul! . . .
I gave jewels for the Madonna's mantle,
And I gave my song to the stars, to heaven,
Which smiled with more beauty.

—*Floria Tosca,* Vissi d'arte

EPILOGUE

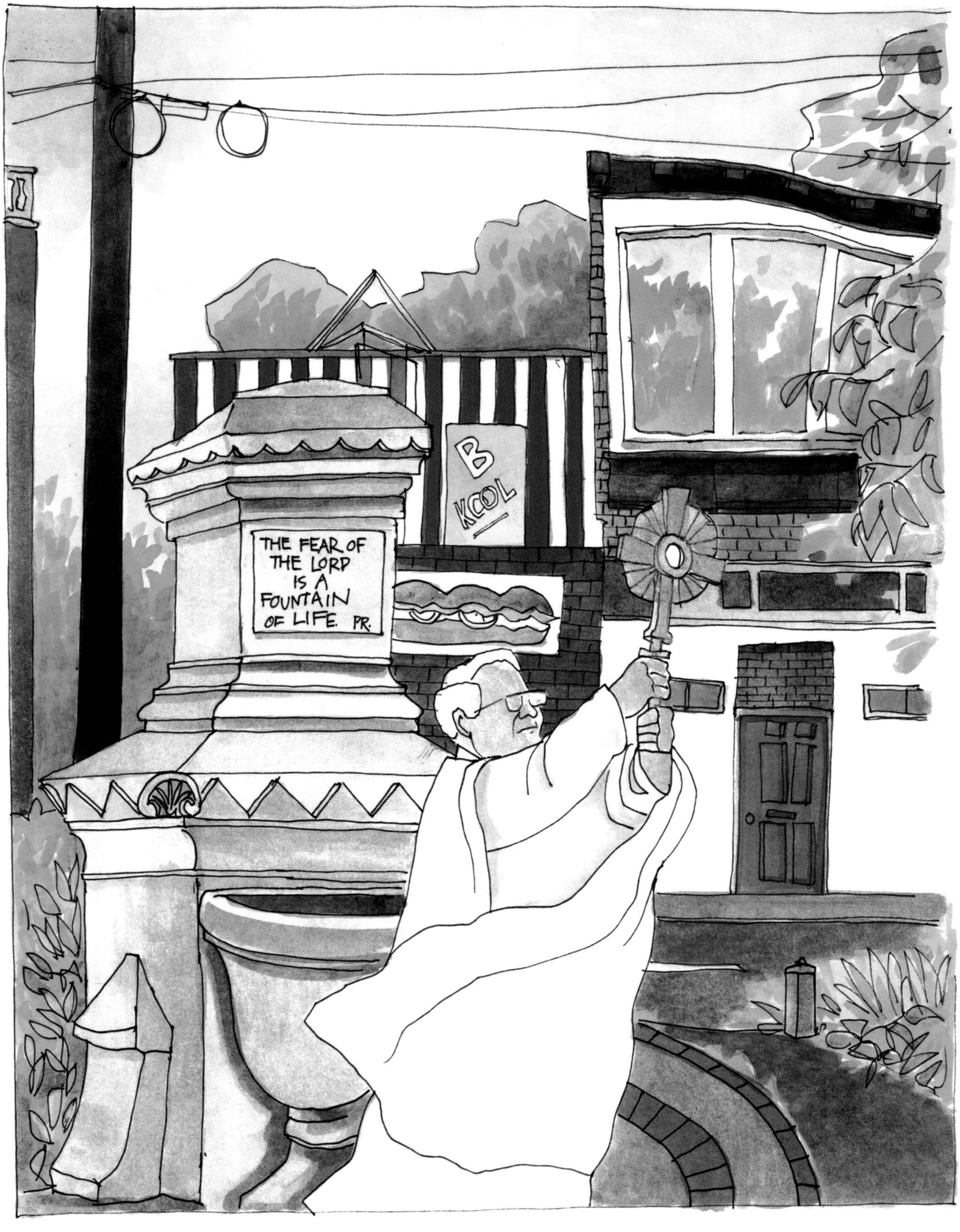
THE FEAR OF THE LORD IS A FOUNTAIN OF LIFE. PR.
B KOOL

The Body of Christ in Camden

O Savior of our souls, we eternally sing, "Live Jesus! Live Jesus, Whom I love! Jesus I love, Jesus Who lives and reigns forever and ever. Amen."

—*Francis de Sales*

Heaven is a banquet, and life is a banquet too, even with a crust, where there is companionship. . . . We are not alone any more.

—*Dorothy Day*

Last year I brought my sketchbook to Sacred Heart on the feast of Corpus Christi because I knew there would be a procession after Mass from the church to a small public square across the street on Broadway. It used to be a dilapidated mess of a corner overgrown with weeds and trash. No one ever noticed the marble water trough for horses that has stood so elegantly in the center of this small patch of earth for a century and a half. That is, until Father Doyle and friends transformed it into a lovely urban garden with a specially commissioned bronze sculpture of "Peace" at the entrance.

A gentle breeze was blowing on that hot summer day as we sang *Tantum Ergo* in English over and over again until everyone was present. That hymn, I humbly admit, always reduces me to tears of nostalgia for a long-gone Catholic boyhood, and this time was no different. I entered the moment, observing and sketching the scene before me: incense wafting into the smelly air; curious hookers and drug dealers looking on from the sidewalk; a city bus picking up and

discharging passengers; sun-dappled flowers and greenery in the midst of urban blight and decay; poetic graffiti on the boarded-up building across the street that rather boldly proclaims "I shall arise"—and which I had never noticed until now; and a monstrance gleaming like the sun.

When it comes to feast days, you can't get much more traditionally Roman Catholic than Corpus Christi, and I never experienced one as poignant, or as meaningful, as this. I was moved to tears that morning, not out of mere nostalgia, but because I had become—we all had become— agents of beauty. The haunting mystery of age-old tradition came face to face with the ugly desolation of modern Camden, a city that stands as ultimate proof of how greedy, desperate, and sin-sick our world has become.

Voices from the world of traditional, private Catholic devotion blended with those of post-Vatican II social awareness and action, the Eucharist our common bond. That, plus our dogged determination not to give in to despair or dread about the uncertain futures of the Church or Camden, of where each is headed once these uncomfortable times have passed. It is as if we are living in an extended Holy Saturday, an anxiety-ridden time and space between the old, which is dead and buried, and the new, whose incarnation has yet to be announced.

I was acutely aware, as I sang, that just a block behind us was my studio, from whose window I paint and observe the relatively quiet, occasionally insane, life of this neighborhood; and behind it a small farm and a greenhouse bursting with green lushness; and a few doors down, a meditation garden dedicated to poets and writers and all those who seek comfort in words; and just a little farther still, a theater where people come to be assured that they are not alone in their long loneliness. All these gentle reminders of Resurrection glory confirm that there is no other place in life I want to be right now; that I have been called here, right here, to this city with these people at this time to do my little bit, my tiny little bit, of bringing joy and hope and beauty into the world. That everything in my recent life, the grief endured and the successes celebrated, led me here; that a vast network of family, friends, and community, some living, some dead, walks beside me; and a host of heavenly saints led by Francis and Dorothy urges me forward in the race.

I could see Jesus in the monstrance, a gleaming white circle of flat bread, but I also observed him much more clearly in the faces dotting the crowd, old and young, in love and in pain, white, black, and brown, prayerful, jubilant, curious. I think I even spotted Dorothy Day, her white hair braided into a halo around her head, amidst the prayerful parishioners and bone-thin prostitutes. We *were* Corpus Christi—the body of Christ, broken in order to be shared, beauty ever ancient and ever new, gathering in one exultant voice of gratitude and praise around a dry stone water trough thirsting for hope, affirmation, and a reason to be there, to keep doing this in all the tabernacles of the world even until the end of time. It had been quite a while since I felt the goose bumps of God's abiding presence in church, but hearing those familiar words from a distant time, as if for the very first time, brought them out:

> *You have given them bread from heaven,*
> *Having all delight within it.*

Deo gratias.

Thank you, God.

Amen.

Streams of the river gladden the city of God,
  the holy dwelling of the Most High.
God is in its midst; it shall not be shaken;
  God will help it at break of day.

(Psalm 46:5–6)

Appendix

OTHER BOOKS BY MICHAEL O'NEILL McGRATH

WORLD LIBRARY PUBLICATIONS

At the Name of Jesus (with Richard Fragomeni)
Blessed Art Thou (with Richard Fragomeni)
Jesus A to Z
Mysteries of the Rosary
St. Cecilia's Orchestra (with Alan J. Hommerding)

ORBIS PRESS

*This Little Light: Lessons in Living from
    Sr. Thea Bowman*
Women of Mercy (with Kathy Coffey)

SHEED AND WARD

*Journey with Therese of Lisieux:
Celebrating the Artist in Us All*

LITURGY TRAINING PUBLICATIONS

Patrons and Protectors: Occupations, Volume 1
Patrons and Protectors: Occupations, Volume 2
Patrons and Protectors: In Times of Need

SERVICE OPPORTUNITIES IN CAMDEN, NEW JERSEY

If you would be interested in bringing a group of high school or college students or adults to Camden for an unforgettable experience of volunteer service, here are some possibilities to explore through e-mail or Facebook. Each has overnight facilities.

- De Sales Service Works (oblates.org/dsw)
- Camden Center for Environmental Transformation at Sacred Heart Church (camdencenterfortransformation.org)
- The Romero Center (romero-center.org)

FOR MORE INFORMATION ON ST. FRANCIS DE SALES

- Francis's two classic works have been beautifully updated and translated by Bernard Bangley. They are *Authentic Devotion*, a reworking of *The Introduction to the Devout Life* (Shaw Books, 2002), and *Living Love*, a reworking of *A Treatise on the Love of God* (Paraclete Press, 2003).

- *Bond of Perfection,* by Wendy Wright (Paulist Press, 1986), is the beautiful story of the friendship between Francis de Sales and Jane de Chantal. Wright also co-edited Francis's *Letters of Spiritual Direction* (Paulist Press, 1988).

PUBLISHED WORK BY DOROTHY DAY

- *The Long Loneliness* (Harper & Row, 1952), Dorothy's spiritual autobiography
- *From Union Square to Rome* (Orbis Books, 2006), the story of her conversion
- *Loaves and Fishes* (Orbis Books, 1997), the story of the Catholic Worker
- *Thérèse: A Life of Thérèse of Lisieux* (Templegate Publishers, 1979), a biography of the "Little Flower"
- With Francis J. Sicius, *Peter Maurin: Apostle to the World* (Orbis Books, 2004)

- Dorothy's articles for the Catholic Worker are beautifully archived by Jim Allaire on the Catholic Worker website (catholicworker.org).

- Her articles for *Commonweal* magazine have been edited by Patrick Jordan in *Dorothy Day: Writings from Commonweal* (Liturgical Press, 2002).

- *Wisdom from Dorothy Day: A Radical Love,* edited by Patricia Mitchell (The Word Among Us Press, 2000) offers short clips from her writings thematically arranged.

- *By Little and Little: The Selected Writings of Dorothy Day* (Orbis Books, 2005) was edited by Robert Ellsberg.

- Robert Ellsberg has also edited her journals in *The Duty of Delight: The Diaries of Dorothy Day* (Marquette University Press, 2008) and her letters in *All the Way to Heaven: Selected Letters of Dorothy Day* (Marquette University Press, 2010).

WORKS ABOUT DOROTHY DAY

I read everything about Dorothy that I could get my hands on, especially all of the works by her mentioned above, but my favorites about her, to which I returned time and again, are:

- *Dorothy Day: Portraits by Those Who Knew Her* by Rosalie Riegle (Orbis Books, 2003).

- *All Is Grace* (Orbis Books, 2011), a splendid biography by Jim Forest, came out just as I was finishing this book, but not so late that I couldn't rearrange the flowers.

- *Dorothy Day: Don't Call Me a Saint,* a documentary DVD by Claudia Larson (One Lucky Dog Productions).

- Interviews with Dorothy can be found on YouTube.

PILGRIM SPOTS WORTH VISITING

The following places may be of interest in planning a Dorothy Day pilgrimage.

In New York City

- The two Catholic Worker houses in the Bowery where Dorothy spent her last years are still going strong. They are St. Joseph House at 36 E. First Street, and Maryhouse, where Dorothy died, at 55 E. Third Street. You can stop for a cup of coffee or to lend a hand any time and check out Friday evening lectures.

- St. Joseph Church, 371 Sixth Avenue on the campus of NYU, is the church she visited in her Hell Hole days. Nearby, on the corner of Sixth Avenue and Fourth Street, is the spot, now The Golden Swan Garden, where the Hell Hole once stood. A plaque honoring Eugene O'Neill has been placed there.

- 115 Mott Street (between Canal and Hester), currently a Chinese herbal products and beauty shop, was the site of the Catholic Worker from the thirties through 1950, before the neighborhood became Chinatown.

- At 29 Mott Street is Transfiguration Church, one of her favorite places to meditate and the site of Peter Maurin's funeral.

- The Tenement Museum, 108 Orchard Street, offers a fascinating look at what life was like for immigrants during Dorothy's first years in New York.

On Staten Island

- Our Lady Help of Christians Church at 7396 Amboy Road, while not the same actual building, is the site where Dorothy was baptized on December 29, 1927. She is represented in a stained glass window there.

- You can walk the beach along Raritan Bay where her cottages were located. Neither of them still stands, but the water still looks the same!

- Dorothy's grave is in Resurrection Cemetery in Pleasant Plains.

Notes

EPIGRAPH

vii *This world in which we live* . . . Excerpt from *Address of Pope Paul VI to Artists, Closing of Vatican II (December 8, 1965)*, copyright © 1965, *Libreria Editrice Vaticana*. All rights reserved. Reprinted with permission.

FOREWORD

xi *I had been passing through* . . . Excerpt from *The Long Loneliness* by Dorothy Day. Illustrated by Fritz Eichenberg. Copyright © 1952 by Harper & Row, Publishers, Inc. Copyright renewed © 1980 by Tamar Teresa Hennessy. Introduction copyright © 1997 by Robert Coles. Reprinted by permission of HarperCollins Publishers (hereafter cited as *Long Loneliness*).

xi *walking on the beach* . . . Day, *Long Loneliness*.

xii *if we failed to rejoice* . . . Ellsberg, Robert, ed. *Dorothy Day: Selected Writings*. Maryknoll, NY: Orbis Books, 1992. Reprinted with permission.

INTRODUCTORY THOUGHTS

xiii *The flowers which I present* . . . De Sales, Francis. *Introduction to the Devout Life*. Translated by John K. Ryan. New York: Doubleday Image Books, 1989 (hereafter cited as *Devout Life*).

xiii *We have a "rule of life"* . . . Day, Dorothy. *From Union Square to Rome*. Maryknoll, NY: Orbis Books, 2006 (hereafter cited as *Union Square*). Reprinted with permission.

1: TENEMENTS

1 *Serve God where you are* . . . De Sales, Francis. *Thy Will Be Done: Letters to Persons in the World*. Translated by Henry Benedict Mackey. Manchester, NH: Sophia Institute Press, 1995 (hereafter cited as *Thy Will Be Done*). Reprinted with permission.

1 *Because God has given me writing* . . . Day, *Union Square*.

1 *If one must dwell in cities* . . . Day, *Union Square*.

1 *I walked the streets in solitude* . . . Day, *Union Square*.

2: JAIL AND THE RIVERS OF BABYLON

5 *To change the world* . . . De Sales, *Thy Will Be Done*.

5 *You cannot pace the floor* . . . Day, *Union Square*.

5 *We were ushered* . . . Day, *Long Loneliness*.

3: IN THE HELL HOLE WITH THE HOUND OF HEAVEN

9 *During the night* . . . De Sales, *Devout Life*.

9 *Where sin abounds* . . . Riegle, Rosalie. *Dorothy Day: Portraits by Those Who Knew Her*. Maryknoll, NY: Orbis Books, 2003 (hereafter cited as *Portraits*). Reprinted with permission.

10 *No one ever wanted to go to bed* . . . Day, *Union Square*.

11 *I became drunk with the beauty* . . . O'Neill, Eugene. *Long Day's Journey into Night*, 2nd ed. New Haven, CT: Yale Nota Bene, Yale University Press, 2002. Reprinted with permission.

11 *All which I took from thee* . . . Thompson, Francis. *The Hound of Heaven*, ll. 171–173.

11 *black despair and tragic death* . . . Ellsberg, Robert, ed. *The Duty of Delight: The Diaries of Dorothy Day*. Copyright © 2008 by Marquette University Press, Milwaukee, WI, USA. Used by permission of the publisher. All rights reserved. www.marquette.edu/mupress/ (hereafter cited as *Duty of Delight*).

13 *I fled him down the nights* . . . Thompson, *The Hound of Heaven*, ll. 1, 2–5.

4: STATEN ISLAND: IN LOVE WITH LIFE

15 *The truest happiness* . . . Camus, Jean Pierre. *The Spirit of St. Francis de Sales*. Edited and translated by C. F. Kelley. New York, NY: Harper & Bros., 1952 (hereafter cited as *Spirit of Francis*).

15 *seagulls diving* . . . Day, *Union Square*.

16 *Just beyond my little lawn* . . . Jordan, Patrick, ed. *Dorothy Day: Writings from Commonweal* (hereafter cited as *Writings from Commonweal*). "Now We Are Home Again," August 19, 1931. Vol. XIV, 382–83. Copyright © 2002 by Commonweal Foundation. Reprinted with permission. http://www.commonwealmagazine.org.

5: FORSTER BATTERHAM: DOROTHY'S SONG OF SONGS

19 *Our faith should be naked and simple.* . . . De Sales, *Thy Will Be Done*.

19 *The very love of Nature* . . . Day, *Union Square*.

19 *If breath is life* . . . Day, *Long Loneliness*.

20 *He stayed out late* . . . Day, *Long Loneliness*.

6: Motherhood and Conversion

23 *Just as an expectant mother* . . . De Sales, *Devout Life.*

23 *A conversion is a lonely experience* . . . Day, *Union Square.*

7: Hooray for Hollywood

25 *We do not pick* . . . Ellsberg, Robert, ed. *All the Way to Heaven: Selected Letters of Dorothy Day.* Milwaukee, WI: Marquette University Press, 2010. Used by permission of the publisher. All rights reserved. www.marquette.edu/ mupress/ (hereafter cited as *All the Way*).

8: Peter Maurin

31 *Let us be who we are* . . . De Sales, *Thy Will Be Done.*

31 *I was a journalist* . . . Day, Dorothy, and Francis Sicius. *Peter Maurin: Apostle to the World.* Maryknoll, NY: Orbis Books, 2004. (Introduction, p. xvii. Quoted from David O'Brien, "The Pilgrimage of Dorothy Day," *Commonweal,* December 19, 1980.) Reprinted with permission.

9: The Catholic Worker Is Born

39 *We should hide our littleness* . . . *Francis de Sales: A Testimony by St. Chantal.* Edited by Elizabeth Stopp. Institute of Salesian Studies, 1967 (hereafter cited as *Testimony*).

39 *Love in action* . . . Dostoevsky, Fydor. *The Brothers Karamazov.* Translated by Constance Garnett. New York, NY: Random House, Inc., 1976.

10: On the Writing Life: The Written Word

43 *We become like the things we love* . . . De Sales, *Devout Life.*

43 *Writing is an act of community* . . . Day, Dorothy. "On Pilgrimage—October 1950." *The Catholic Worker,* October 1950, 1, 2. *The Catholic Worker Movement.* http://www. catholicworker.org/dorothyday/Reprint2.cfm?TextID=615. Reprinted with permission.

44 *I was all for plunging right in* . . . Day, Dorothy. *Loaves and Fishes.* Maryknoll, NY: Orbis Books, 1997. Reprinted with permission.

44 *I am a journalist* . . . Jordan, ed., *Writings from Commonweal.* "A Reminiscence at 75," August 10, 1973. Vol. XCV. Copyright © 2002 Commonweal Foundation. Reprinted with permission. http://www. commonwealmagazine.org.

11: Art, Artists, and the Spiritual Works of Beauty

47 *The sight of beauty* . . . De Sales, Francis. *Treatise on the Love of God.* Edited and translated by John K. Ryan. Rockford, IL: Tan Publishers, 1975 (hereafter cited as *Treatise*). Reprinted with permission.

47 *We need to bring beauty* . . . Ellsberg, *All the Way.*

47 Image based on a drawing by Ade Bethune held in the Ade Bethune Collection, St. Catherine University Archives and Special Collections, St. Paul, Minnesota. Used with permission

48 *Ade Bethune's drawings* . . . Day, *Loaves and Fishes.*

48 *One couldn't help loving Dorothy* . . . Eichenberg, Fritz. *Works of Mercy.* Maryknoll, NY: Orbis Books, 2004. Reprinted with permission.

50 Image based on a drawing by Ade Bethune held in the Ade Bethune Collection, St. Catherine University Archives and Special Collections, St. Paul, Minnesota. Used with permission

12: The Garden State

51 *The church is a garden* . . . De Sales, *Treatise.*

51 *God is our creator* . . . Day, *Long Loneliness.*

13: The Saints

55 *Choose particular saints* . . . De Sales, *Devout Life.*

55 *I get so impatient* . . . Ellsberg, *Duty of Delight.*

56 *Charity consists* . . . *Story of a Soul: The Autobiography of Saint Thérèse of Lisieux.* Translated by John Clarke, O.C.D. Copyright © 1975, 1976, 1996 by Washington Province of Discalced Carmelites, ICS Publications, 2131 Lincoln Road, N.E., Washington, DC 20002-1199, USA. www. icspublications.org. Reprinted with permission.

56 *We can measure our love* . . . Day, Dorothy. "From Union Square to Rome, Chapter 13—Your Three Objections," 152–173. *The Catholic Worker Movement.* http://www. catholicworker.org/dorothyday/reprint2-cfm?Text ID=213. Reprinted with permission.

56 *It is happier* . . . Ellsberg, *All the Way.*

58 *Where there is no love* . . . Ellsberg, *All the Way.*

58 *In the presence of angels* . . . Excerpt from *The New Jerusalem Bible* copyright © 1985 by Darton, Longman & Todd Ltd. and Doubleday, a division of Bantam Doubleday Dell Publishing Group, Inc.

14: Miserere: Forgiveness Seventy Times Seven

59 *My dealings with people* . . . Camus, *Spirit of Francis*.

59 *No matter how corrupt* . . . Ellsberg, *All the Way*.

60 *Poor widows* . . . Camus, *Spirit of Francis*.

61 *As a convert* . . . Ellsberg, *All the Way*.

15: Peace, Popes, and Protests

63 *Nothing should have the power* . . . Stopp, *Testimony*.

63 *We are not asking God to deliver us* . . . Day, Dorothy. "In Peace Is My Bitterness Most Bitter." *The Catholic Worker*, January 1967, 1, 2. *The Catholic Worker Movement*. http://www.catholicworker.org/dorothyday/Reprint2.cfm?TextID=250. Reprinted with permission.

65 *No more war* . . . Excerpt from *Address of Pope Paul VI to the U.N. General Assembly, Oct. 4, 1965,* copyright © 1965, *Libreria Editrice Vaticana*. All rights reserved. Reprinted with permission.

65 *If you want peace* . . . Excerpt from *Message of His Holiness Pope Paul VI for the Celebration of the Day of Peace, 1 January 1972,* copyright © 1971, *Libreria Editrice Vaticana*. All rights reserved. Reprinted with permission.

16: Love and Kindness

67 *We must do all through love* . . . De Sales, *Thy Will Be Done*.

67 *If we could only learn* . . . Ellsberg, *All the Way*.

17: Practicing the Presence of God

73 *May God live in my heart* . . . Stopp, *Testimony*.

73 *We must practice* . . . Day, Dorothy. "Aims and Purposes." *The Catholic Worker*, February 1940, 7. *The Catholic Worker Movement*. http://www.catholicworker.org/dorothyday/Reprint2.cfm?TextID=182. Reprinted with permission.

75 *the early morning sun* . . . Day, Dorothy. "On Pilgrimage—December 1978." *The Catholic Worker*, December 1978, 2, 6. *The Catholic Worker Movement*. http://www.catholicworker.org/dorothyday/Reprint2.cfm?TextID=594. Reprinted with permission.

75 *Setting up the loom* . . . Ellsberg, *Duty of Delight*.

18: Beauty and Music

77 *Calm your mind* . . . De Sales, *Thy Will Be Done*.

77 *St. Bernard says* . . . Day, Dorothy. "On Pilgrimage—April 1953." *The Catholic Worker*, April 1953, 3, 8. *The Catholic Worker Movement*. http://www.catholicworker.org/dorothyday/Reprint2.cfm?TextID=649. Reprinted with permission.

78 *One must search for beauty* . . . Ellsberg, *Duty of Delight*.

19: Aged Beauty

81 *I keep feeling my heart* . . . Stopp, *Testimony*.

81 *If God wills the work to go on* . . . Riegle, *Portraits*.

81 *Do forgive this awful typing* . . . Ellsberg, *All the Way*.

82 *I'm sleeping and writing* . . . Ellsberg, *All the Way*.

83 *Night holds no terrors* . . . Excerpt from the English translation of *The Liturgy of the Hours* © 1974, International Commission on English in the Liturgy Corporation. All rights reserved.

20: The Church Ever Ancient, Ever New

85 *I am expecting a great storm* . . . Stopp, *Testimony*.

85 *Heaven is within you* . . . Ellsberg, *Duty of Delight*.

21: Death and Funeral

89 *Everything done for love* . . . Stopp, *Testimony*.

89 *It all happened* . . . Day, *Long Loneliness*.

89 *She loved us* . . . Riegle, *Portraits*.

21: The Body of Christ in Camden

95 *O Savior of our souls* . . . De Sales, *Treatise*.

95 *Heaven is a banquet* . . . Day, *Long Loneliness*.

Brother Mickey McGrath is a painter, writer, and speaker who loves to make connections between art and faith. He lives in Camden, New Jersey, but offers presentations and retreats around the country (to any group that will listen) on the healing and prayerful power of beauty. *Saved by Beauty* is his sixth book created in collaboration with World Library Publications.